NEPALI WOMEN RISING

PRATIVA SUBEDI

Published by :

Women Awareness Centre

Kathmandu, Nepal
P.O. Box 2245
Phone : 417355

English edition : June 1993

© author

Price: NRS 150.00
US$ 4.00

Printed at :
Sahayogi Press,
Tripureshwar, Kathmandu, Nepal
Tel : 211489

Table of Contents

Comments on the Nepali Edition of this Book

Women should have strong determination and honesty while raising any issues concerning women, as rights can only be attained through struggle. The number of women representatives in parliament is quite limited, but all the women dedicated to fields related to women's welfare should be always prepared to demonstrate in the street and to stage protests in front of the parliament in order to achieve our economic, social and political rights and social justice as well as to end discriminatory laws. Those of us who are in the parliament are ever ready to give you a helping hand. This book is a positive contribution in the field of women's awakening.

Shailaja Acharya, Minister for Agriculture
(At the book releasing ceremony)

This is a very useful and informative book written with much careful study. It is extremely readable and will undoubtedly contribute to women's awakening. The writer's efforts are commendable for she has honestly expressed her conclusions on the position of women in our society and the way they are treated in our male dominated society.

From a book review in **Deshantar** Weekly 29 March, 1992

Prativa Subedi has contributed this readable work to the Nepali society by using her talented pen for women's awakening.

From Book review in **Janamanch** Weekly, 19 March 1992

The burning problems of injustice, oppression and exploitation of women in different fields have been minutely studied in this book. The author has addressed the real issues of women in Nepal.

Kapil Ghimire, **Madhuparka,** May 1992

This book gives one an idea about the status of women in our society and the fundamental issues regarding women. It reflects her deep study of various problems and conditions as regards women at large. The book is a comprehensive presentation of burning issues concerning women in our country.

Shree Gautam, **Gorkhapatra** Daily, May 2, 1992

From the author

Prompted by feelings bubbling inside me I started writing about Nepali women, but when I actually began working among the communities of poor women in rural areas I was even more determined to speak and write about the lives of these women. While living and working in different communities I saw life there in increasingly difficult conditions despite continuous hard work. I saw the one-room thatched huts that sheltered all the family members in one corner and their cattle, goats and sheep in another. I saw how the people survived - on the meager grains they could cultivate on the steep slopes and terraces and on whatever they could find in the forests, their morning and evening meals earned by endless labor. And I saw that most of the responsibilities towards the house and the family as well as the agricultural work fell to the women.

Whether in villages, towns or cities, the life of most of the women I saw was a struggle against the odds. Deprived of opportunities, I saw women who lacked self-confidence in their own inherent skills and capabilities. But I also saw women who developed self-confidence when they were given even a few opportunities. The situation of women in our country is slowly improving, although we have a long way to go.

I hope the thoughts and realities I have expressed here will help the women understand their own contribution, capacity and power to rise. I wanted to share with women in other countries the situation of Nepali women who have had their self-esteem suppressed for so long, but still they are rising.

In the process of writing this book I received tremendous support from many individuals of various organizations and friends. I am indebted to Gretchen Martin for her tireless effort in both editing and putting this manuscript on the computer. My thanks also to Rosemarie Cecchini and Jenny Sowerwine for their assistance in editing, and to Tara Nath Sharma for his translation. I express my sincere gratitude to Phoebe Ravenhall, whose encouragement over the years has been a constant source of inspiration. My thanks also to Surya Subedi for his encouragement and spirit.

April 1993   Prativa Subedi

Chapter 1

WOMEN AND SOCIETY

In perpetuating the continuity of creation it is said that women and men complement each other. In actual fact, however, it is a lopsided relationship with the woman performing the roles of protectress, nurturer, healer and guide. Nepali women are daughters, wives and mothers, but are not recognized as individuals with their own identity, despite the fact that they are as human as men. Society has relegated women to the lowest rank and to a submissive role, confined to the home and farm and their responsibilities there due to their maternal function. They are discouraged and prevented to take part in public life.

A complex society like ours with a multiplicity of religious and cultural traditions and a variety in family structure does not easily permit us to generalize about the status of women in Nepal as such, but it can be stated without reservation that Nepali women from the communities high in the Himalayan region to those of the lowlands in the southern terai region are exploited and oppressed.

From her very birth the girl child is discriminated against, often seen as an unwanted addition that somehow must be tolerated until she can be married off. Her emotional growth is suppressed by values imposed by family and society until she is emptied of her most natural human qualities, a girl without a personality or the capacity to think independently. Now she is fit for marriage - a girl who knows her duties, but not her rights. Seldom is she informed of the few rights which she is allowed within the legal framework. One of the most fundamental rights, however, that of equal inheritance, is completely denied her so she is dependent on her father as a child, on her husband after marriage, and on her sons in her old age.

There is no difference in the intrinsic natures of a newborn baby girl and boy. It is not that a girl is passive and a boy active from the moment of birth. It is during the process of their upbringing that very definite restrictions are imposed on the girl's activities. From the very beginning the qualities of shame, fear, passivity and dependence on others are instilled in girls. The natural human qualities of being active, courageous, curious, conscious, self-reliant independent and spirited are completely destroyed. The mind and mental make-up of the girl is prepared according to what the society expects of her before she has even grown into her youth, in order to prepare an "ideal" woman as prescribed by society's norm.

Our society is made up of many cultures and sub-cultures, but it is the Hindu culture that is the most influential, especially with regards to defining the role of women. In ancient Hindu society women like Apala, Ghosha, Vishurabara, Ramasha, Lomasha, Sachi all contributed stanzas to the Rig Veda, the most ancient religious scripture of Hinduism. There were learned women like Gargi and Maitreyi who were famous for their stimulating discourses. There were also women sages such as Sulabha, Anusuya, Arundhati, Lopamodra and Ketaki who obtained great power through meditation. Women were considered to be the symbol of power, prosperity and knowledge, and were represented by the goddesses Mahakali, Mahalaxmi and Mahaswarswati. Up until the present people have paid respect to these goddesses in the temple, but not to the everyday woman in her home.

In Hindu scriptures there is on the one hand a glorification of womanhood and on the other a degradation of woman. Some passages show that women were highly respected, and honored, such as the following:

"The gods rejoice where women are worshipped."[1]

While other passages, were derogatory, for example:

"By nature a woman is deceitful and pushy, a liar foolish and greedy. She's impure and she's cruel."[2]

Values and attributes accredited to women were perpetuated through stories, poetry and song. Individuals motivated by self-serving interests and fundamentalists who did not want to see women as capable and strong, laid

---

[1] Manusmriti. The Manava Dharma Sastha or law book of Manu is often known as Manusmriti. The prose sutras were expanded and remodelled in verse form from the second and third centuries A.D. Manusmriti is one of them.

[2] Chanakya. Name of a minister of Chandra Gutpa (c. fourth century A.D.) reputed author of Chanakya Shloka which are written on morals, and principles of government and society. This saying reflects the attitude towards women in his time.

2

the foundation for unjust practices in the name of culture so that the gender relationship between women and men became imbalanced. Differences between their social roles grew more complex. For example, there is a book called Swasthani which is very popular in our society. In fact, it is read every evening in the month of Magh (mid-January to mid-February) in homes all over the country. It tells of a 70-year old man named Shiva Sharma who marries a 7-year-old girl named Goma. She soon becomes a widow and her miserable life as a widow is glorified, thus encouraging women to follow the very strict rules that restrict the life of a widow. The scriptures admonish the woman in her role as wife as follows:

"However he may be: useless,
A womanizer and bastard
The woman must worship
Always as a god her husband"[3]

Sons are viewed as protectors of and providers for the family. Daughters are viewed as the future property of another. Sons can open the gates of heaven for their parents by performing prescribed rituals after their death. A daughter has no such power. There is a strong belief in our 'raditional families that parents will gain merit by giving their daughter in 'riage before her first menstruation. About 50 years ago a daughter would spena only four or five years with her parents before she would be sent to her husband's family, and even for that brief duration her parents would worry about how to relieve themselves of their burden.

A stanza from a famous epic reflects the joy of the parents who have just handed over the responsibility of their daughter:

"The daughter is a thing to give away
For someone else she is kept
What a relief to send her away today
I'm light as a feather and free from debt."[4]

These lines were written about 1600 years ago, but this attitude still persists today even in our so-called educated circles, and even more so in the rural areas. Child marriage is still prevalent. One of the major problems in

---

[3] Manu-Smrti, see footnote 1.
[4] Kalidasa's play "Abhigyanashakuntal", 4th century A.D., translated into English by Shambhu Prasad Dhungel.

3

our society is our inability to think critically about values that have been thrust upon us since ancient times.

Girls are still taught from an early age that they are impure during their menstruation and for 11 days after childbirth. In fact, a girl's first menstruation is marked by a period of complete isolation from the male members of the family and community. Instead of explaining the natural changes that will soon take place in her body, her guardians put her into a dark room where the sunlight is completely blocked out so that the sun god (representing masculine energy) may not see her and be polluted by her "impure condition". In this way she is taught to internalize shame - shame for her own body and its most natural function. This practice is accepted by Brahman, Chhetri and Newar communities and even by families of other ethnic groups influenced by Hinduism. Sometimes Newar families will place the girl in a dark room before she reaches puberty, then when the first menstruation takes place she need not go into confinement again.

Unfortunately it is the women in our society who perpetuate this practice and emphasize the difference in gender roles to such an extent that it can create a real gap between a boy and a girl who in childhood had developed a mutual friendship. With this socially imposed segregation girls are set apart - in a negative way - and are more apt to be teased, harassed and victimized.

In the past and still even today, in order to maintain their social prestige, the victim and her guardians conceal rape cases because of the importance for an unmarried girl to remain pure and virgin, but now, with more openness about rape cases it is known that young girls as young as five years old, married women, as well as women as old as 60 have been raped. A constant sense of fear is created in young girls to convey to them the necessity of protecting their virginity.

Not only does the girl live with a fear of rape, but there are other fears she must live with which are due to misconceptions about her body, menstruation and pregnancy. In early puberty it is common for menstrual periods to be very irregular; not menstruating for months at a time is not uncommon. Many girls who have had no sexual contact whatsoever, may fear, out of ignorance and misinformation, that they might be pregnant if their period does not come one month. In some cases they will go so far as to elope with a classmate - not necessarily even a boyfriend - because they believe that somehow, by mere touching, or even thinking, they have

4

become pregnant. Such can be the consequences of ignorance and misinformation.

As in many male-dominated societies, women in our society are taught to be what they "ought to be" rather than to develop their own unique selves. Consequently they lose their spontaneity and even their identity. All of their natural expressiveness is suppressed by rules and social norms, an example of which can be seen in poet Bhani Bhakta Achrya's "Instructions to a daughter-in-law":

> Women should not laugh, only whores do so
> And the housework will never get done.

To further illustrate the dictates of expected behavior for a woman, poet Achrya refers to two situations in the following lines: one, where a man's two wives must live together and two, to the practice of "sati" where a woman is expected to commit suicide by throwing herself onto the burning funeral pyre of her dead husband.

> "Being each the wife of one husband
> It's a sin to get mad at each other
> Whatever it is, whenever he dies
> You'll have to jump into it together"

Such expectations are still prevalent in our society, except for the system of "sati". The sati system is no longer practiced, but the expectation is still prevalent that women must control and even deny their feelings even in the most extreme situations.

A further illustration of the denigration of women can be found in "Ram Charit Manas", regarded as a great poem of Hindu literature. It refers to women in these words:

> Drums and idiots
> Outcasts, beasts
> And women are fit
> Only for beating.

This defamatory idea has contributed to a widespread misconception that women are incapable of ever reaching the level of men. Such literature discouraged even raising the question of the equality of the sexes.

5

Yet in other scriptures woman is respected and praised. In one ancient text, woman is referred to as the creator of the universe and the universe is in her image. She is the supreme being of all the beings. There has never been and there will never be (anyone) with such a destiny equal to that of a woman.

These contradictory ideas about women have led to much confusion as to woman's image of herself and to others' conception of her. Unfortunately, it is the negative stereotyping of women which has predominated. The time has come for women and men to wipe out gender stereotyping.

It is the scriptures that have provided the basis for our patriarchal society. There are two main schools of thought with regards to the scriptural origins of our patriarchal system: (1) that they are man-made and, hence, it is possible to gradually change them; and (2) that they are god-made, and since god has created woman for man, there is no possibility to question male dominance. It has been so ordained.

The socialization of girls and women in a male dominated society has had such a great impact on women that they, in turn, consciously or unconsciously, enforce the patriarchal system. Therefore, women are exploited not only by men but by women too, and even by themselves by accepting and internalizing those demeaning values from the scriptures and the society which is based on them. Women are now starting to work together, but they still have a long way to go before they are really united. Our patriarchal society has encouraged a "divide and rule" policy, which has discouraged the development of any real sense of sisterhood.

Even in a patriarchal society some women may reach the top political position - Indira Ghandi, India; Benazir Bhutto, Pakistan; but still they have difficulty in bringing change in the discriminatory laws.

The characteristics of our patriarchal society have resulted in clear patterns and structures subordinating women. These include:

a)   Restrictions on educational opportunities
b)   Misrepresentation in the media
c)   Control over women's productivity
d)   Family control over women's reproductive power
e)   Control over women's mobility
f)   Control over parental property

g) Discriminatory religious practices
h) Discriminatory legal system
i) Economic restrictions

Each of these points is elaborated on below.

(a) Restrictions on educational opportunities

The majority of girls are deprived of an education because they are required to help their mothers with the chores, consequently they leave school at an early age, if they go at all. The common attitude is that education for girls is a wasted investment. If educational expenses for children must be cut down because of economic difficulty, the daughter is the first one to be withdrawn from school. In the process of providing opportunities for education, health and other basic necessities, mothers are unlikely to treat their sons and daughters equally because their ideas and attitudes are similar to those held by most people in a male-dominated society. Failing to assert themselves freely, they have, with the passage of time, internalized all the ideology and values of the patriarchal system. In bringing up their own children, the women express the same ideas and values that were present when they were brought up and treat their children in the same way as they had been treated. Only a limited number of women, those who are self-confident and are proud to be a woman, treat son and daughter equally. The majority of girls, who are deprived of the basic human rights in life, such as the right to education, are forever handicapped and cannot make use of the opportunities made available later on by the social, economic and political system.

(b) Misrepresentation in the media

Most of the communication media present two images of women. One as the traditional dedicated housewife, the other as a sex object. Immediately after encouraging women to become ideal housewives by buying the best quality soap, a TV commercial will next use sexy women to sell a food product. Because men dominate the communication media, priority is rarely given to news items, information, and activities particularly related to women. In our context the communication media plays a negative role both by manipulating woman's image in a totally distorted manner and by undersupplying pertinent news items.

(c)   Control over women's productivity

Men have defined what is "work" and how work is valued. All that women do at home is not defined as "work" per se, and so it is not given any economic value. What work women may do outside the home is often valued lower than men's labor of equal value. In addition, the head of the family, who is male, may control every aspect of her work, including where she works, the income she earns, and how she uses her income.

(d)   Family control over woman's reproductive power

It is expected that every woman will marry and have children. According to Hindu religious custom, it is the son who must look after his parents in old age or in infirmity, and it is he who offers prayers and rituals after their death in order for them to be assured a place in heaven. Therefore, until the mother gives birth to a son, her place in her husband's family is not secure. She must continue to produce children until the family is satisfied with the number of sons she has produced. It is the mother who is of greatest importance in childbirth and child rearing, yet it is the father's name which is given to the child.

(e)   Control over women's mobility

Women are allowed to go out in public during the day time. The social norms imposed on women, however, make many of them hesitant to walk, work, or talk freely to others in public. Due to a constant fear of having their character and reputation spoken ill of, many women feel safe only under supervision and do not go out alone. Men definitely have much more mobility than women. The difference in the freedom of movement is due mainly to the disparity in their upbringing.

The dress for men and women is very different. Women cannot move freely not only because of the social restrictions imposed on them but also because of the bulky, burdensome clothing they are bound to wear.

(f)   Control over parental property

A daughter cannot lay claim to parental property. Because only sons inherit the father's property, a woman is first a temporary dependent in her parents' house and then becomes a permanent dependent and maybe even a refugee in her husband's house. In our society there is no fixed address for a woman until she becomes somebody's wife and up until that time she may not own property.

(g)   Discriminatory religious practices

Most religious customs are favorable to men. In our context the Hindu theologians have described the duties of men and women in religious scriptures. Most of the worship and prayer rituals are performed by men. For example, the naming ceremony for a baby is not done by the mother but by the father, or one of his brothers. Furthermore, the presence of a male member of the family is obligatory in the ceremony. Hinduism dictates that marriage is for bearing children and, most important of all, to have sons.

(h)   Discriminatory legal system

Our laws have been influenced by religious texts which favor men. Even our new constitution was prepared by a committee made up of men only and the laws affecting women are still highly discriminatory.

(i)   Economic restrictions

Work is often determined on a gender basis. Women are given jobs that pay less or they are paid less even when the job is equal to that of a man. Women have very little opportunity to make financial transactions on their own as they do not have ownership rights.

9

Today, although transformations may have come about in our manners, speech and dress, as we have seen in many of the points presented above, we are not very far away from the situation which prevailed in ancient times. The main obstacle that continues to block recognition of women's full potential stems from obstinately held narrow concepts regarding women. In a patriarchal society the position of a woman is that of a second class citizen. This does not mean that we now advocate the necessity of a matriarchal society. Rather we envision a human society of men and women where the personality of one sex is not dominated by the other. The mere difference in physical structure does not make it necessary for one sex to lose complete human identity and live in surrender to the other sex. Harmonious coexistence should be the guiding principle in the relationship between man and woman and not as if one were a slave and the other his master. Therefore, it is essential that every woman and every man, each in his/her own sphere, contribute to removing the discrimination, exploitation, and oppression of women on the basis of sex. Everyone's effort is necessary to make people in our society realize the importance of mutual partnership and harmonious coexistence and the mutual benefits which will come from such a partnership.

Men must readjust their opinion of women. A man is often impressed by and admires any intelligent, dynamic woman, as long as she is not his own wife. This double standard exists in all classes of our society. Even educated men tremble to hear expressions like "feminism" and "women's liberation" when in actuality all they are really concerned about is "Who will wash my socks?" They need not be afraid. The feminists believe that relationships should be based on mutual respect, justice and equality and are concerned with bringing our lopsided relationships into balance.

Chapter 2

WOMEN AND TRAFFICKING

The illegal trade of women and young girls for prostitution is a wicked social crime. The widespread implications of this trade have appeared as a dangerous problem and a major challenge. In our country this problem has taken on terrible dimensions. In the prostitution houses of India the number of Nepali girls is approximately 172,000.[1] According to different researchers, 5,000-7,000 Nepali girls are sold every year in India alone. Not only are they easily taken across the border, but they are also trafficked inside Nepal itself, despite the fact that prostitution and trafficking are illegal both here and in India. (Although in India prostitution is "tolerated" in specific red-light areas.) A large number of these girls and young women come from rural areas, especially from the districts of Kabhre, Sindhupalchok, Nuwakot, and Makawanpur, yet this problem is really countrywide.

Most of the traffickers are themselves Nepali. These agents usually take the girls to the various red-light districts located in Bombay, Calcutta, Lucknow, Banaras, and Madras. The majority of these unfortunate young women leave for India in the expectation of having a comfortable life. The agents have lured them to India with promises of marriage, or wonderful opportunities: of employment, to meet their husbands who have gone into the army, or to become actresses in films. Few girls opt for this profession willingly. Those who go are mostly victims of social injustices (a polygamous marriage) who are despised or abandoned (by husband and family), and those already devastated by poverty. They are innocent, ignorant, and ambitious, easy prey to allurements.

The process of women trafficking has evolved in different ways. During the Rana regime, girls were brought from different parts of the country to serve as attendants, servants, and cooks in their palaces. Many of

---

[1] "Bal Sarokar", CWIN Newsletter No. 10, Child Workers in Nepal, 1992.

them were used as objects of recreation and sexual pleasure. They were employed as mistresses or kept as wives.

During the Second World War, employment was available for Gorkhas in the British Army, as it still is. The comings and goings of people from every part of the country for army recruitment centers provided a pretext for agents to take Nepali girls to the Indian prostitution markets.

Later, after the Revolution of 1951, which overturned the 104-year Rana regime, many rulers and high-placed palace people migrated to India taking many of their female attendants with them to keep them as mistresses. As time passed these girls no longer lived in the luxury they had previously enjoyed. With the hope of continuing their easy and comfortable life these former Rana attendants were compelled to enter the marketplace and sacrifice themselves to prostitution.

The present day trafficking in women has tarnished our glorious national image. Every day more of our young women are lost. Not only are these girls exported, but this illegal trade has thrived inside the country also in big and small hotels.

Parents, husbands, brothers, and uncles are involved in the selling of the innocent female members of their family. The girls are forced to submit to the trade in spite of their reluctance and many of them are unknowingly kidnapped. We know actual cases of girls and young women of villages who were sold by members of their own families.

For example, a 12-year-old Tamang girl who lived in Nuwakot was promised by her own uncle that he would arrange a job for her as a carpet weaver, but instead took her to a house of prostitution in Bombay. She was rescued by the Indian police and returned to Nepal. According to her, she had no idea that she was being taken to be sold into prostitution.

Another example is of a Brahmin woman who was taken to Calcutta by her husband where he sold her, then ran off. She cried, shrieked and shouted, and with the help of a security guard working in the brothel itself, she was successful in escaping. After corresponding with her relatives back home, she was able to return with one of her relatives who went there to bring her back. If she had any inkling of the intention of her husband to sell her into prostitution, she would not have agreed to go with him to Calcutta. She has since remarried.

Another Tamang woman who was also sold by her husband, was taken to Bombay. She said that she did not want to stay and ran away. On her escape she was met by a policemen and admitted as an unpaid worker into Asha Sadan, a women's shelter in India, where protection is provided for a few years to young women up to the age of twenty, with a view to rehabilitating the former prostitutes of Bombay. She explained that she returned to Nepal because she did not wish to stay in Bombay without any income.

A twenty-year old girl from Sarlahi District has returned from Bombay's red-light district. The following explains how she was sold and then managed to escape. When she was at the market of Bayalbas, a neighbor, Satya Lama, proposed marriage to her with all kinds of promises. Then he told her that he had a job in Delhi and persuaded her to run off with him to Bhajaipur in India. (All the while he told her that he was taking her to Delhi to marry her and start his job.) There they stayed for a night in the house of his friend. Then he took her to Bombay to another friend's house, Usha Kiran Vishwakarma, and, on the pretext of going to see the market, he left her with Usha Kiran and, unbeknownst to her, returned to Nepal. Then Usha Kiran said that they should go in search of Satya Lama and took her to prostitution house no. 13-730 in a lane in Bombay and sold her for Rs. 25,000. After she had been living a life of torture there for two months, she was hired for sexual services for two months for Rs. 18,000 by Jahir, an Arab. While she was staying with the Arab, she told him her tragic story. He paid twenty-five thousand rupees on her behalf to the prostitution house and took her to Patna where he left her with her cousin, giving Rs. 7,000 for her keep. She was successful in returning to Nepal. After her return to Nepal on July 9, 1991, she saw Arjun Bahadur Gole whom she recognized as belonging to the women trafficking gang at Bardibas Chowk. Previously, she had seen him talking with Satya Lama in India. She reported him to the police and he was arrested. According to the police, Arjun Bahadur Gole told them everything, about how he was the leader of Usha Kiran's woman trafficking group and how he had accepted IC 25,000 for this job when he went to Bombay.[2]

In another incident, Miss Kumari Gurung from Haibung village of Sindhupalchok district described what she saw with her own eyes. "A mother, for the purpose of earning money, forcibly sold her pregnant

---

2   Nepali Patra Weekly, July 31, 1991.

daughter under the threat of death. The young pregnant woman was raped in a Bombay brothel where she died. Even though the mother knew about her first daughter's death, she sold her second daughter also."[3]

And so it is that our daughters and sisters are being sold. From 1960 to 1970 most of the victims of this illegal traffic were girls between the ages of 18 and 19, but since 1970 most of the girls have been between the ages of 11 and 14.[4]

Our society has traditional practices that have helped to continue this sex trade. A semi-nomadic community, the Badis are found in many districts of the Rapti, Bheri and Seti zones of Western Nepal. Badi families used to move from house to house and from village to village singing and dancing to make their living, but with the onset of modern films and video cassettes, their old tradition of singing and dancing for entertainment had to be changed to suit the demands of the time. Since it was hard to make both ends meet with dancing alone, they gradually switched over to prostitution. Some Badi women have settled down permanently in towns to be engaged in prostitution all year round, but most of them come down to the terai towns with their families for prostitution. After making some money they return to their mountain homes.

There are about 30 families of Badis living in Nepalgunj as permanent settlers. The women of the Badi community are permitted by their husbands and family members to carry on with the profession of prostitution openly. In the Badi community families desire to have female babies. The girl is initiated into prostitution first at home and gradually she starts to visit clients' houses or big hotels, according to the demand. A girl 15-20 years of age earns, on average, Rs. 1,000 daily. Among her usual clients are policemen, army men and other government servants, as well as Indians from across the border.

Religious superstitions are at the very root of the Deuki system. In almost all the districts of Mahakali Zone, and in some districts of the Seti Zone, girls are offered to the gods at temples, even to this day, in order to obtain one's cherished desires. A girl is offered either by buying somebody's daughter or by giving one's own daughter to the Goddess or to one's family

---

3   Durga Ghimire: "The Illegal Trade of Sisters and Daughters", a paper presented at a conference of the same name, Kathmandu, October 31, 1990.

4   Jyoti Sanghara: "Terror in the Indian Brothels".

14

god at the temple. After they are offered the girls grow up in the local temple. They are known as Deukis. Some of those who have offered the girls take care of their food and clothing for a short time, but as the girls grow up, the limited income resources of the temple are inadequate and they are bound to practice the sex trade just to maintain themselves, having already been "initiated" by the priests.

Their religious customs do not permit these girls to marry. In addition, there is a widespread superstition that intimate sexual relations with a Deuki will bring eternal bliss, which naturally further encourages the practice of prostitution. It is estimated that there are about 19,000 Deukis and 17,000 Badi women now regularly involved in prostitution.[5]

In the same way, in the Himalayan region, girls of the Sherpa community are also offered to the Buddhist temples under the Jhuma custom. When they grow to maturity, they have sexual relations with the Lamas. Their sons will later become Lamas there.

Those who have actually seen the girls at various prostitution houses in India report that they are subjected to terrible physical and mental torture in their early days until they submit themselves. Those who are successful in escaping describe the systematic process of torture. Their stories are heart-rending. Some of the inhuman practices against these young women are to lock them into a dark room, slap and beat them, starve them, put snakes under their beds to frighten them, threaten then rape them. Finally, it is so unbearable for them that they submit and are raped by a number of men. Some of the girls being prepared for a life of prostitution are thus raped by several men at a time and die due to excessive torture.

The superstition still persists that if a man with venereal disease has sexual intercourse with a virgin, he will get well. With that hope in view, several men get in line for the competition, each trying to outbid the other for the opportunity to rape a virgin girl.

The women who act as pimps, agents and madams are more beastly and cruel than the monsters of folktales. They do not care whether the girl is underage, pregnant or sick. All are delivered to the monsters' hands. They keep them while they are young enough to continue the commercial

---

5   Mahesh Shrestha, Asmita (Women's Magazine), Issue 10, December 1990.

transactions, then drive them away when their youth is gone. Those who are prepared for the sex trade have to satisfy up to ten clients every day. The clients are usually fully intoxicated and therefore the girls, too, like to be intoxicated. The madam keeps all their income for herself until their original cost is reimbursed. After her initial investment is realized every prostitute gets Rs. 25-30 per client, but they must share half of that amount with the madam. The girls are forced into the sex trade, even before their natural age for sexual intercourse. It would appear that human civilization has come to an abrupt end in such places. These girls are made to stay in the prostitution houses while they have youth, beauty and health. After that they have to live on the streets and byways and may even be prepared to offer their body for five rupees. In the Kamachhipura area of Bombay there are about 660-700 prostitutes on the footpaths. Many are Nepali women. "In the southern streets of Bombay there are many insane women who were at one time involved in prostitution. These are the ones who could not adjust to their surroundings or circumstances. Most prostitutes suffer from hysteria, mental diseases, despair and depression."[6]

Most of the women engaged in prostitution suffer from venereal disease. Some of these sexually transmitted diseases are incurable. According to researchers these women often go to quack doctors rather than to qualified physicians. An even more terrible situation is that 25%-30% of the women involved in prostitution are infected by the H.I.V. positive virus,[7] and when this is discovered, they are thrown out of the brothels. Some of these women return to Nepal, others stay behind and live along the footpaths. Those who return to Nepal arrive in a terrible condition. They return with many kinds of diseases including the fatal one, AIDS. Women returning from Indian brothels are sure to be ousted by society and if they are the victims of AIDS, they are despised and scorned even more. Many of them, therefore, conceal the AIDS disease and thereby infect others, who will themselves also face death.

When one suffers from mental imbalance, even a small disease takes on enormous proportions, and due to lack of good medication all diseases become more complex. Once these women are attacked by AIDS, there is no way out for them. It is indeed pitiful to see these women who have had to

---

6 Savarang Jansatta (newspaper), Dr. S. C. Mackenzie, September 9, 1989.
7 Ibid.

undergo such cruel social injustices and physical torture in their life with no other option than to bear their suffering alone until death.

Nepali girls in the thousands are sold like beasts every year, being lured by false promises of a comfortable life. According to our country's law, the trafficking of persons is a criminal offense. Laws against sex trafficking are very strict, but application of the law is very weak. As a result the law exists merely on paper. In Section 11, Clause 1 referring to the crime of trafficking persons the Nepali Code of Laws stipulates:

"No individual shall take any person by temptation out of the territory of Nepal with the intention of trafficking. If the individual is arrested before selling the person being taken to a foreign land, he or she will be imprisoned for ten years, but if the victim is already sold, the culprit will be imprisoned for twenty years. If the purchaser of the victim is found inside the territory of Nepal, he or she will also receive a penalty equal to that of the seller. Those who support such a crime knowingly will receive half the penalty of the main culprit."

Although the law has fixed equal penalty for both the seller and the buyer, this crime is still increasing in society. This is because of the inability to identify the criminals spread throughout the country. Also those who are arrested escape the penalty because they deposit large sums of money as a bribe. It is clear that the administration and the criminals reach a common understanding that allows them to go free. Another problem, of course, is the open border between Nepal and India which allows such freedom of travel between the two countries and easy escape from one country to the other.

Police inspector Om Bikram Rana, explained the problem this way at the seminar, Illegal Trade of Sisters and Daughters, October 31, - November 1, 1990, Kathmandu: "There is a practical difficulty in arresting and charging an individual before the actual crime, only on suspicion. If in doubt, an individual can be interrogated at the border. The girls in their company have no knowledge that the individuals are criminals who will sell them and then vanish. Therefore, the girls take the side of the culprits. They tell the border police that the individuals taking them to be sold are their relatives. The girls, even after being warned that they are being taken for prostitution, do not realize or believe it. We cannot arrest anyone just on suspicion."

But even in the process of being rescued and returned to Nepal, several cases have come to light in which the rescued girls were raped by the police themselves. This is an example of a male mentality which believes these girls can be treated as inhumanly and as cruelly as possible. It was reported in the Nepali newspaper that on October 9, 1990, a 19 year old girl, who was under the custody of the police in Butwal district, was raped by three policemen.

There is also much oppression and sexual violence by the police in India. A pitiful case is reported by researcher, Jyoti Sanghara, who was present in a brothel (that held 600 prostitutes) at the time it occurred. During an interview with a woman in one of the rooms, suddenly there was a loud commotion. On investigation, the researcher saw many naked girls in one room. Clients were also present at that time. About two hundred policemen had poured into the brothel in a surprise raid. They left after emptying the pockets of the clients. Prostitutes who gave money to the policemen were allowed to stay behind in the house, but those who had no money were taken to the police station and consequently to prison. After some time the arrested girls were released and brought back to the brothel by the madam.[8] This kind of terrorizing is a common occurrence in their lives.

In Thailand, commercial sex is big business and everyone, from politicians to local police, has a share in the profits. The government does not want to lose valuable dollars from tourists who come for sex, sun and the sights. "Two-thirds of the five million tourists who visit each year are male and 20% are single men from nearby Malaysia and Singapore."[9]

In Thailand, many married women who are not prostitutes are at risk in having sexual relations with their husbands because of the danger of contracting the AIDS virus from them. Women have a greater risk of contracting AIDS from men than men do from women because men travel so much more and are more likely to have other sex partners. It is estimated that at least 1.5 million Thai women will be HIV positive by the year 2000, and so will one-third of their children. "If we don't change our sexual behavior drastically," says government minister and AIDS activist Mechai Viravidya, "it will be hard to find an AIDS free man in ten years."[10]

---

8   Jyoti Sanghara, "Terror in an Indian Brothel."
9   Newsweek, June 29, 1992.
10 Ibid.

18

Trafficking has increased between developing and developed countries. Women of poor countries, especially, have been lured to developed countries for job opportunities or marriage. Poor Asian women are lured to Japan in large numbers. These women are then forced into the sex trade in hotels, bars and brothels. Every year about a hundred thousand women go to Japan, among whom are those who go for jobs legally, as well as those going illegally. About 90% of them are Filipinos, Thais and Taiwanese. All of them become involved in prostitution.[11]

These women are obliged to work as captives once they are brought to Japan by the dealers and agents. They are not in a position to oppose any kind of inhuman treatment. After it became known that many of these women committed suicide, women's groups and organizations began to protest. In 1983 during Prime Minister Li Kuan Yu's government, about 3,000 Thai prostitutes were sent back to Thailand from Singapore. In 1981 the women of Japan and the Philippines jointly demonstrated in front of the Japanese Prime Minister during his visit to Manila. In spite of such protests, the unjust, exploitative system of selling and buying women increases worldwide.

There are about two hundred marriage agencies in Germany which import Asian women to western countries. After the number of battered women married through such agencies increased, the Philippine government declared illegal from June 1990 onwards, all clubs and organizations that arranged marriages to foreigners through mail order brides. The culprit is supposed to receive a prison sentence of 6-8 months and be fined Rs. 20,000.[12]

In Bangladesh, before uninitiated girls enter into prostitution, they are ritualistically "married" to the master of the prostitution house. They begin to take clients for sex immediately afterwards. Most women involved in prostitution encourage their own daughters to enter the profession. Some of them, however, first send their daughters away to get an education. There are great social and economic differences among the prostitutes. A woman who engages in prostitution at her home in the capital city of Dhaka was found to

---

11 Yayori Matsui, "Asian Migrant Women and the Sex Industry in Japan", In God's Image, June 1990.

12 "Mail Order Brides of the Philippines", Prabodha Newsletter of CWRS, Sri Lanka.

have earned up to 15,000 Banglaldeshi Takas from one customer, whereas a woman in a common house in the red-light district receives only 15 Takas from each of her clients.

In Bangladesh there is a rehabilitation program for those who can escape from the red light district. However, though women receive food and a place to stay for some time, they do not like to remain there for long. Again they return to prostitution because they cannot mix freely in a society that rejects them. As Zarina R. Khan explains, "The reason why women continue in prostitution is not only due to poverty. Therefore economic programs alone cannot solve this problem.[13]

In our society women are looked upon as objects of enjoyment. From birth and early childhood many unnatural values are imposed on the girl as she is prepared to go to another's house. She is denied education and other basic requirements. She is unable to appreciate or understand her own capabilities and human potential. She knows only how to follow someone else's directions. Because of her ignorance everyone takes unjust advantage of her and she becomes abused and exploited - so much so that she may even be sold by her own family.

Most of the trafficked girls are from the lowest income groups. In order to attract the girls of poor families into the sex trade, female pimps visit the villages dressed in expensive clothing. Nepali families which are struggling to exist at even a subsistence level economically have begun the practice of earning quick and easy money by selling their sisters and daughters. Morality is the loser in the fight with a hungry stomach.

About 17.5 million people in Nepal live in rural areas and are deprived of even the basic amenities. The literacy rate is 36% for the population at large and only 18% for women. The effect of poverty is felt by all men, women and children, and yet it is the women and girl children who suffer the most. Education is very necessary, for it is the source of knowledge. Formal education and the experiences gained therein help a person to become mature and aware. Education also develops sound judgment and good character in a human being.

---

[13] Zarina Rahman Khan, "Prostitution in Bangladesh", Manushi (magazine), no. 56, Jan.-Feb. 1990.

The situation has been favorable for traffickers because of the lack of commitment on the part of political leaders in fulfilling their electoral promises to ensure the rights of their constituents - especially women. Every year hundreds of girls are exported like cattle, but politicians seem to take the enormity of the problem very lightly, paying no attention whatsoever and raising no question even when concrete evidence is found in their own constituency. Now in the open atmosphere it is urgently necessary for the democratic government together with those involved in social organizations - particularly those concerned with women - to take action against the trafficking of women.

Despite the gravity of the problem, our communication media has not played its expected role of creating awareness among the general population through publicity and broadcasting. In order to encourage people to eradicate this evil once and for all, the efforts of individuals and institutions must be boosted up by the communication media. This should be done without compromising the privacy and dignity of the victims, such as publishing their photos and names without their permission. In this regard, the media must play a responsible role; the trafficking of women is not an issue for yellow journalism.

The Women's Welfare Home, which was set up by the Ministry of Labour and Social Welfare in 1985, provides shelter and training in sewing and knitting for nine months for 20-25 girls from underprivileged areas in order to help them become self-supporting. Formerly, a quota of 5 seats were reserved for girls rescued from prostitution, but unfortunately since fiscal year 1990-1991, these girls can no longer be trained in this home.

A social organization called ABC Nepal (Agro-Forestry, Basic Health and Cooperatives) held a seminar on "The Illegal Trade of Our Daughters and Sisters and Our Responsibility" on October 31 and November 1, 1990. It was able to draw the attention of governmental and non-governmental organizations and institutions, policy-makers, political leaders and social workers by bringing them all together to address the problems. Other organizations active in issues concerning trafficking are the Creative Development Center (CWD), Child Workers in Nepal (CWIN), and Center for Women and Development (CWD).

It is relevant to present the superficial rescue efforts made in India. For the purpose of rescue in January 1990, the police made a raid on a red light district of Bombay and from the various brothels, 854 women and 85

21

children were "rescued" and dumped into the open air prison of Madras. The policemen contacted the families of those whose addresses could be traced in order to hand over the girls to them. Many of the rescued girls wanted to go back to their homes, but their parents did not want to accept them. The parents did not want to cause obstacles to their other children's marriages and they feared the loss of family prestige. AIDS tests were given, often using only one syringe for many women. Two-thirds of the women were found to be HIV positive. It cost the Indian government IC 10 million annually to take care of these women. Such an approach is neither practical nor compassionate. Therefore, efforts should be made to create an atmosphere in which the girls will be accepted by their families. Other efforts are needed to stop the trafficking of women and to carry out preventive measures to keep girls from being exploited by the traffickers and the police.

Many women who spend a traumatic life in prostitution houses give birth to children there, willingly or unwillingly. Beds are separated by cloth curtains like those in hospitals, with the clients and the children present in essentially the same place. Many mothers keep their children sedated with intoxicating drugs when the clients arrive. If the children are a bit older, they are sent to roam the streets. Most Nepali mothers in the brothels do not send their children to school. According to researchers the mothers fear that they might get lost when sent outside to study. Children who are sent to school do not stay there long. They are rejected by classmates who tease them because their mothers are prostitutes. Only a negligible number can study and are sent far away from the house of prostitution to boarding schools or to stay outside in private apartments. Most girls are obliged to follow the same course as their mothers, so few can get out of the trap of prostitution. The children are denied all human rights. Although it is extremely difficult to bring up these children, women involved in prostitution still have a desire to have children.

Measures to be taken in order to deal with the problem of trafficking:

- Awareness raising. Preference should be given to programs that help develop awareness in girls so that they know they have as equally an important role as boys to play in society. Organizations, and institutions must work to change these attitudes through training and action-oriented programs.

- Amendment of laws. Implementation of the present day legal system is very weak. As there is no procedure for imposing punishment on the criminals on the complaint of a victim, the individual merely becomes one more in the large number of victims and the crime is then easily concealed. There should be necessary amendments in the law in order to facilitate implementation.

- <u>Formal and informal education.</u> Sufficient information should be provided to young people and adults through the formal and non-formal curricula about the actual condition and adverse effects of trafficking. Through both formal and informal education, efforts should be made to create self-confidence so that everyone in society is aware of his/her responsibility in the prevention of this crime. Unless people are able to resist the lure of the sex trade, the question of helping others does not arise.

- <u>Publicity.</u> Both the governmental and non-governmental communication media should give priority to information about trafficking as much as possible, especially regarding the criminals, in order to discourage this crime. Strictest confidence, however, must be maintained with regards to the victim.

- <u>Political and social commitment.</u> There is a great need for the commitment of all educated people, including social workers, social organizations and political institutions established for the rights and interests of women, to stamp out trafficking. Having brought the criminal to the attention of the people, the authorities should be pressured to enforce strict legal action.

- <u>Temporary rehabilitation.</u> The girls who have returned after having been rescued should be provided temporary shelter, health care and guidance. It is necessary to make arrangements for adequate training to enable them to begin a new life. Those who want to come back to Nepal from India should be brought back.

- <u>Employment.</u> Many of the girls and young women are sold via the Nepali carpet and garment factories. Therefore, efforts should be made by social organizations, institutions and government agencies to provide alternative employment opportunities, especially in socio-economic problematic areas.

- <u>Exchange of ideas.</u> Among various governmental and non-governmental organizations and institutions, there should be an exchange of ideas in order to discourage and prevent the trafficking of women and a campaign should be started for this purpose. Dialogue should also be started with the concerned counterparts in India.

No single individual or organization can put a stop to this problem. It is enormous and it is growing by leaps and bounds. This indeed is not a problem of a particular class or a particular area. It is rather the concern of the whole society. Therefore, everyone's participation is of paramount importance to do away with this evil once and for all.

Chapter 3

WOMEN AND THE ENVIRONMENT

Human beings are interrelated with all other living things in the environment. The health of Mother Earth is sustained when there is harmony between human beings and their environment. But to fulfill their needs, human beings have been using the resources of the earth non-stop and without consideration as to the consequences. As a result, there has been great destruction to our environment. Pressure on our natural resources has grown on a massive scale. The activities of man are responsible for the depletion of forests, creation of deserts, and the erosion of the soil, which then leads to floods, landslides and the loss of valuable topsoil. Industrial waste products are poisoning our water sources and deadly fumes are polluting the very air we breathe. All this has resulted in the depletion of the ozone layer, which has led to the "greenhouse effect", which threatens the very existence of all living creatures. We do not need the scientists to tell us that if man fails to receive the affection of Mother Nature by taking care of the earth, the result will be the extinction of all life here. In this situation one cannot afford to think of the development and progress of mankind without the protection and preservation of our environment. Every year acres of forest and jungle are destroyed bringing about the extinction of innumerable species of plants and causing the earth's temperature to rise thus posing a serious threat to the earth's life support system. If the abuse and consequent deterioration of the environment continues in this way, mankind will soon vanish from the face of the earth.

In Nepal's context, deforestation, increased land requirements because of uncontrolled population growth, land erosion and landslides are some of the main causes of rapid environmental deterioration. Industries are being set up haphazardly in the urban areas. Without paying any heed to the effects of environmental pollution, all kinds of industries producing paper, leather and fabric goods, soap, alcohol, sugar and beer as well as carpets - only to name a few - are dumping their by-products (chemicals and toxic wastes) anywhere, thus polluting our sources of water - the rivers, as well as our wells and main water pipelines. These industries are partly responsible for the environmental degradation and are creating serious irreparable health hazards.

Our drinking water is seriously affected. In a recent study, one milliliter of the drinking water distributed through pipes in Kathmandu was tested and shown to contain 30,000 germs which can lead to the spread of many diseases like cholera, diarrhoea, jaundice, typhoid, dysentery, etc. Sewage drain pipes empty directly into the rivers and ponds, which is one reason why innumerable contagious diseases are so rampant.

According to the 1991 census, the population of Nepal has reached 18,462,081, with an annual growth rate of 2.1%. The effect of such rapid growth on the environment is obvious. There is massive clearing of forests for new settlements, fodder and firewood are cut for use or for sale. The trees and their by-products were the only source of national income until just a few decades ago.

Before 1955 more than 50% of the land area of our country was covered with forests, but by 1964 it had decreased to 45% and by 1978 to 38%. The panchayat regime, desperate for money so that they could defeat the democratic forces at the referendum of 1980, cleared massive forest areas and sold the trees across the border. Again in 1989, during the deterioration of Nepal-India relations when kerosene could not be imported, the same government cleared huge forest areas for firewood.

Even during the fourteen months of the interim government (1989-1991) after the establishment of democracy, deforestation took place at an alarming rate, and it still continues unchecked. From February 1990 to May 1991 alone, the data published by the government show that trees covering an area of 35,655 bighas were cut down.[1] According to government statistics 37.5% of the land area is still covered with forests,[2] but according to forest experts a more reasonable estimate is that in actuality only 20% of our forests remain. According to environmentalists, in order to maintain an ecological balance, at least 43% of all land should be covered with forests. Even though many reforestation programs have been implemented, the size of our forest areas is still decreasing.[3] As the forests in Nepal are depleted,

---

1   Report, Ministry of Forest HMG, 1990.
2   Ibid.
3   Economic Survey (1989-1990), Finance Ministry, HMG.

the country is facing a formidable challenge to preserve and protect that which is left as well as to establish massive reforestation programs.

The main causes of the destruction of forests are:

-	Deforestation for expansion of agricultural land
-	Use of firewood for 87% of fuel requirements
-	Use of wood in the ever-growing construction industry
-	High-handed-ness of licensee contractors
-	Illegal export of wood
-	Lack of political commitment in forest conservation
-	Lack of consciousness of the general public about the importance of forests
-	Imposition of projects from "above" as opposed to developing projects in accordance with the wishes of the people, and often without the people's participation
-	Exclusion of women in forest conservation activities

While formulating objectives, policies and programs concerning forestry, the government passed laws and regulations without any heed to popular participation and consequently their implementation remains ineffective. On the one hand, common peasant families were prevented from collecting firewood for their basic daily requirements, while on the other hand those with political or other influence could acquire government permission to export wood.

Although the concept of community forest development was formulated decades ago, rural women have not been included in the development schemes. Under the programs specified for women, only a few have been included in nurseries, tree plantation, plant production and the construction of smokeless stoves.

Every year more and more of the world's tropical jungles are being destroyed. Valuable trees like sal and teak, which were in abundance in the terai (the Nepal plains), have been cut down with impunity, irrespective of the fact that one sal tree requires 60 years of growth before being suitable for use as timber. A notable point is that these trees can grow only in a subtropical climate, such as that of the terai. The deciduous forests - with deodars, walnut and paper-making trees that grow between 4,000 to 10,000 feet above sea level, and the coniferous forests - where red rhododendrons and other similar trees and plants grow, have been largely destroyed. Forests are the green lungs of the earth, and we need them to breathe. Because of the destruction of forests in our mountainous regions floods, landslides and soil erosion have increased, creating devastating conditions that are often irreversible.

Every year the erosion of arable land in Nepal is increasing. In our country there are altogether about 6,000 rivers. In the rainy season they cut into the banks with such force that our rich, fertile top soil is carried by the rivers to Bangladesh and India. According to a study conducted by ESCAP, between 1981 and 1986 approximately 12,300,000 trees were destroyed in Asia. By 2000 AD it is estimated that 70% of the forests in Asia will have been destroyed. With the destruction of the trees comes the loss of the soil. In Nepal, due to soil erosion and floods, about 240 million square meters of fertile soil are lost annually, as a result of which the level of the rivers in the terai has risen by 15 cm to 30 cm. And again due to the severe destruction of forests, the rivers in the terai constantly change their course, removing soil from one bank and adding sand to the adjacent fertile land on the other.

Rivers take their own courses, but when dams are constructed on them the rivers sometimes flow right through the middle of settlements. Large areas of fertile cultivated land are thus destroyed.

For example, the Koshi Agreement made between Nepal and India on April 25, 1954 which resulted in the construction of a huge dam, has turned hundreds of hectares of arable land in the adjacent areas of the Koshi into marshlands.

Before constructing other dams, the welfare of the people should be put far above everything else and consideration should be made on how the dams will affect the local communities both now and in the future.

Furthermore, dams can be damaged by earthquakes and other natural disasters causing unimaginable devastation. The Himalayas, the youngest mountain range in the world, are also the weakest, and therefore have the greatest chance of earthquakes and landslides. Because of these earthquakes and landslides the mountainous soil is eroded in large quantities. In 1978 there was a landslide 10 km long on the Bhagirathi River (which is considered the largest river in the Ganga Basin) despite the fact that there was a good catchment area around it and heavy forestation on both banks. In the same manner there were as many as 20,000 landslides along the Tista River in 1986 alone. Two hundred years ago the Tista merged with the Ganga, but now it runs into the Brahmaputra. Within the last 250 years, the Koshi River has changed its course by 120 meters.[4]

Unfortunately, our government has just made a deal with the World Bank to build the Arun Dam which will destroy huge tracts of forest and farm land. This present project will benefit experts and engineers only, not the people. Rather than constructing huge hydro-electric projects in Nepal on the Arun river, Pancheshwar and the Karnali rivers, small hydro-electric projects should be established all along our river systems.

According to a reference made in a report on India's environmental condition by an Indian organization called the Centre for Science and Environment, 3/4 of all the land in India suffers from floods. The increasing floods in Assam and the Ganga Basin in India are caused mainly by the landslides in the mountains of Nepal. Critical problems of this dimension can only be solved with the understanding and cooperation of all the countries concerned.

Women are the primary users of forests and consequently should be considered their primary conservationists. For example, it is women who are responsible for collecting firewood, fodder, and plants and roots for food and medicine. In our context 78% of the firewood is collected by women, and 6% by girls, bringing the overall collection of firewood by womenfolk to 84%[5]. As for the role of men, they carry the forest products to distant markets and sell them. It is the women who are the forest gardeners, sowing the seeds and planting the trees, weeding and watering them and caring for their growth. We must make use of women's skill and knowledge for the development and conservation of forests, and include them in the planning and design of forestry programs.

The Chipko Movement of Uttar Pradesh in India is a dramatic example of how women have contributed to forest conservation. When contractors came with their government licenses to cut down the trees, the women there put their lives at stake when they embraced the trees and faced the contractors. The Chipko Movement began on April 24, 1973. Their

---

4 "Myths on Himalayan Floods Demolished", The Times of India, October 4, 1991.
5 Status of Women, CEDA (Centre for Economic Development and Administration), Nepal, 1981.

29

leaders were Sunarlal Bahuguna and Chandi Prasad Bhat. This movement succeeded because of the active participation of women. Among the women leaders of this movement were Meera Behn, Sarala Behn, Bimala Behn, Hima Devi, Gauri Devi, Ganga Devi, Vachani Devi, Itawari Devi and Chamun Devi. Along with them were many other women who also played important roles in that movement.[6] They participated in the movement because the women of that region had seen their land ravaged by floods and landslides. After their dramatic step, the government did not permit the cutting down of local trees without the permission of the local population and in addition, it began a tree plantation campaign. This movement demonstrated courage, strength and determination on the part of women for the preservation of their forest environment. Because of the Chipko Movement no sawmill was set up in that area. Sundarlal Bahuguna, an environmental activist, said that a few years ago he would have given consideration to the establishment of a sawmill for the economic development of the mountainous region, but today he clearly sees that to put up a saw mill in the area would be to strip Mother Earth naked, as the sawmill would go on digesting trees in its belly until the whole forest was completely destroyed forever.[7]

Malaria was eradicated in the Nepal terai region in 1964. After that, settlements grew up where jungles once abounded. It was necessary for people to construct houses to live in so they felled the trees to make their homes. Then, in the name of development, sawmills were set up, jungles were cleared and timber was exported without restraint. Even today with the alarming deterioration of the environment, the rivers are drying up, the timber trade is growing and the sawmill owners are felling trees in ever increasing numbers. Financial gain from the use of forest products continues to increase at a tremendous rate. Negative effects touch all people, but especially so the women who now have to go even greater distances to collect firewood, fodder and water.

When difficult circumstances arise for the male members of the community they can go elsewhere in search of jobs, but women and children are bound to stay at home to face the situation. Any development which brings more difficulties than benefits is maldevelopment. A change in the whole philosophy and process of development is necessary and we have to think of practical ways of bringing about this change. In community development the participation of women should begin at the local level, and

---

6   Vandana Shiva, "Staying Alive", Kali for Women, 1988.
7   Ibid.

this should be kept in mind by workers in both the governmental and non-governmental fields. Those who make decisions should bring about a positive change in their decision-making process. In any of the village programs which have been initiated only those which have community support and involvement have proved to be long-lasting. Development workers, having seen the positive results of programs which were carried out with the participation of women, have begun to discuss the need for women's participation in their own activities. Women are the main consumers of environmental resources and they are the direct victims of environmental destruction.

The negative impact of the ecological imbalance on agriculture has forced people in the rural communities into non-agricultural professions, often resulting in the men leaving the village to look for work in the cities. Unplanned, unrestrained urbanization has added enormously to our environmental problems. Basic human needs like housing, clean drinking water, management of sewerage and a mass transportation system are not available to the majority of people. Whatever facilities are available are concentrated only in the urban areas. Trade and industries are established in large towns only, but without adequate planning. All kinds of industries are operating in the middle of heavily populated areas, dumping their wastes into the rivers, open fields and into the air without any treatment to remove toxicity and impurities. The health of the people and animals is compromised, the fertility of the soil is lost, and the vegetation too is contaminated.

The Kathmandu Valley suffers from such environmental problems. Countless industries, such as the Jawalakhel Distillery, the Bansbari Leather and Shoe Factory and the carpet factories - particularly those engaged in washing and dyeing - have been polluting our environment by dumping their chemically poisonous waste materials haphazardly. The dust blowing from the Himal Cement factory has caused respiratory diseases among the people living in nearby villages, and the constant blasting at the Godavari marble quarry has upset the whole ecological balance of a once-great forest area.

The government must make and enforce stringent laws regarding industries and give urgent attention to zoning laws. Furthermore, each industrial estate, should have waste water treatment plants to ensure that the water that irrigates our fields is safe.

31

Nepal is also making its contribution to the Greenhouse Effect. The earth is surrounded by atmosphere. Among the various levels of atmosphere the level closest to the earth consists of various gases in a mixed form which are essential to the living world. These gases are nitrogen, oxygen, argon, carbon dioxide, etc. There is a blanket of gas which acts as cover in the atmosphere which is composed of molecules consisting of three atoms of oxygen and is known as the ozone layer. This ozone layer provides protection to all living beings and vegetation on earth because it prevents the penetration of harmful ultraviolet rays of the sun from reaching the earth. It protects living beings by shielding them from the harmful effects of these rays. In the last few years, because of environmental imbalance, there has been destruction of part of the ozone layer and consequently the ultraviolet rays have been able to penetrate to the earth and more and more people have been stricken by skin cancer. The damage to the ozone layer was discovered by pictures taken by a satellite named Nimbus-7 in 1979 which showed a hole in the ozone layer in the atmospheric layer above Antarctica. "The scientists are of the opinion that the loss of the ozone layer is caused by gases of the chloroflorocarbon class coming from earth. Chloroflorocarbon is composed of chlorine and fluorine mixed with carbon dioxide."[8] Chloroflorocarbon is used as the propellant in aerosol cans (hair spray, deodorant, insect spray etc.), as well as in the coolant of refrigerators and air conditioners. In this way the gases and chemicals used on earth reach the atmosphere and are destroying the ozone layer. It was only when this problem came to be known that 46 developed countries, including the USA, Japan and Russia, which produce goods containing chloroflorocarbon, agreed to immediately decrease their production and use of this chemical by half and to stop its production altogether by 2000 AD. Even the developing countries like India and China have agreed to stop their production by 2010.

Because of human infringement upon the natural system the air was polluted the atmosphere was damaged and the earth's temperature began to rise and it is still rising. This warming of the earth is called the Greenhouse Effect. With an increase in temperature comes the melting of the polar ice regions. By 2100 it is estimated that the sea level will rise by 1 meter,[9] in which case some countries in the middle of the ocean, like the Maldives, are in danger of being submerged. This Greenhouse Effect is due to the increase the amount of carbon dioxide in the atmosphere. While it is true that some of it comes from natural events like volcanic eruptions, most of it is

---

8   Buddi Bal Shrestha, Gorkha Patra, August 3, 1991.
9   Kiran Shankar Yogacharya, Gorkha Patra, June 5, 1991.

produced by use of carbon-based fuel, deforestation, chemical waste materials and the pollution produced by factories and mills.

In this way the inhabitants of all the developed and developing countries are contributors to the Greenhouse Effect and to other forms of environmental degradation as well. Environmental pollution in developed countries is mainly due to industrial and nucleur waste while in developing countries it is mainly due to an inability to control the growing population which sustains itself by destroying natural resources. The population of the world has reached 5,300,000,000 of which about 1 billion live in developed countries. These people are using the natural wealth in large quantities and are destroying the ecological balance.[10] For the past twenty years various meetings, gatherings, studies and research have been conducted on the subject of the earth and the necessity of maintaining an environmental balance. The conclusion has always been that human beings together with all other living things will be unable to survive on this earth if sufficient attention is not given to natural conservation.

An international conference on the environment attended by 178 heads of state and government officials was held in Rio de Janeiro, Brazil on June 13 and 14, 1992. The most comprehensive meeting of its kind ever to be held. The conference discussed the future of the earth with a view to concluding treaties on biodiversity and prevention of deforestation under Agenda 21 by mobilizing the necessary resources. To implement Agenda 21, the United Nations estimated that poor countries would need $125 billion each year in aid, or $70 billion more than they are now receiving.[11] The conference adopted a resolution 800 pages in length under Agenda 21. The United States did not sign the Biodiversity Preservation Treaty, which was aimed at safeguarding animals and living things which are disappearing from the earth. The American delegation argued that it could not stop its assistance to thousands of industries which provide employment opportunities and aid to poor nations of the world. The Rio Convention has emphasized women's role in the ecological management and development of the environment and concluded that their full participation is necessary for responsible development in this area.

---

10 Caring for the Earth: A Strategy of Sustainable Living, The World Conservation Union, the United Nations Environment Program and the Worldwide Fund for Nature, October 21, 1991.
11 "The Road from Rio", Newsweek, June 22, 1991, p.12.

The earth, which is our home, has been unhealthy because of a heavier burden than its natural resources and means can carry. No particular nation or individual is to blame for bringing about this situation, but the time has come when all nations, each according to its capacity, must come forward to mobilize and lead the people in the direction of environmental conservation. Human beings are the main contributors to environmental degradation. In recent times, in order to care for the earth with a view to balancing the environment, governmental and nongovernmental organizations and agencies on national and international levels have come to a consensus. The following are the policies proposed for implementation on a world wide basis:[12]

- Respect for our life-supporting system and taking care of it
- Improvement in the standard of living
- Conservation of earth's life forms and its variety of species
- Decreasing the destruction of non-renewable resources
- Remaining within the carrying capacity of the earth
- Bringing a positive change in individual attitudes, styles and behaviors
- Enabling the common mass to conserve their environment
- Making national schemes available to unify development and conservation
- Laying the foundation of mutual cooperation on a worldwide scale

Most of the nations have decided to implement the above-mentioned points in their own national projects. In the context of Nepal, the economic development of the hilly region is an utmost necessity in order to implement these policies and will, in turn, decrease migration to the terai. The distribution of land in the terai region should be just, fair and equitable. Without efforts to eradicate poverty, environmental protection is not possible. In our situation the destruction of trees and vegetation is the only means of survival for many people because of abject poverty. Until and unless there is an improvement in the living standard of the poor people, there is no way that environmental protection can be accomplished in Nepal. Conservation comes second to a hungry stomach.

---

12 Caring for the Earth: A Strategy of Sustainable Living, The World Conservation Union, the United Nations Environment Program and the Worldwide Fund for Nature, October 21, 1991.

A priority in ensuring environmental protection is to begin to raise the level of awareness of the common people. Those communities which have already experienced floods and landslides have started to conserve their forest areas. Prevention, however, is better than cure, and awareness raising campaigns should be carried out before the environmental balance is hopelessly upset. In all forestry programs women's participation is essential. Without the support and participation of all the people no program can be successful.

An important factor in environmental degradation is the overuse of the natural wealth of timber and firewood, the supply of which is almost depleted. Tree plantation and protection campaigns, either on an individual or community basis, are urgent measures to be taken. Information about the interdependence between plants, animals and humans, has to be disseminated to the general public for the good of everyone.

Unfortunately, the total apathy of the Ministry, Divisions, and government organizations concerned with forest protection has resulted in the near extermination of the forests. Encroachment into the forest areas has not yet been stopped. Furthermore, government officials and contractors actually conspire to make use of forests for personal and economic benefit. The present government should discontinue this practice immediately. If the government is incapable of making and enforcing rules and regulations, this kind of highhandedness will grow all the more. Forest destruction was a problem in Thailand, Indonesia, Japan and Malaysia as well, but now because of strict government policy and stringent measures, stealing and exporting timber has stopped altogether. To solve this problem these countries put several laws into effect and enforced them.

As already mentioned, huge tracts of forest land were destroyed for political interest during the time of the National Referendum, and the Interim Period, but even after the achievement of democracy this madness has continued in the same haphazard way. Who will lead the people in forestry conservation? The people have a feeling that forests are government property. To encourage the people to feel more personally involved we should emphasize the development of community forests. Another feeling of most of the village people is that it is not worth planting trees for timber, firewood and fodder because they do not bring an immediate return. Most of the rural people are of the opinion that no investment should be made on things that do not give fruit immediately. Again, the poor peasants do not have sufficient land. Therefore, the public media should disseminate information as to how the slopes and edges of fields can be best utilized. Through concerned agencies and organizations programs should reach the people at the local level. Since most people are illiterate, especially the women, publicity should be in the form of visual materials, films, and posters.

Both the small and large nations are equally responsible for the deterioration of forestry and environmental degradation. The rich countries silently import, on a regular basis, the priceless timber and natural wealth from developing countries. European companies made huge profits by importing timber from Asian countries on a large scale. The priceless timber of Nepal was stealthily smuggled into India in huge quantities and this illegal activity is still going on. Therefore, environmental protection requires not only the efforts of governmental and nongovernmental agencies and organizations, but also cooperation at the international level as well.

Chapter 4

WOMEN AND EDUCATION

The meaning of the word "education" is derived from the Latin word "educatus" which denotes a gradual process of taking an individual from ignorance to the primary stage then through various levels of knowledge acquisition. From the earliest beginnings of human society the process of learning has existed in some form. In the ancient Vedic period, the system "Gurukul" or teacher-disciple relationship was in practice, but as the centuries rolled by, the demands of time brought changes in the process of teaching and learning. But then as now, the fundamental purpose of education has always been the development of the individual and the enhancement of knowledge. Education is the only basis for developing inherent qualities of an individual. It is a natural right for human beings to have equal access to education which is, in fact, the foundation of civilization and the measuring rod of development. Education in modern times should be productive and readily available to all.

Illiteracy is a serious problem today. Over one hundred million children in the world are debarred from the opportunity of primary education and 960 million adults are illiterate. Of these figures two-thirds are girls and women. How can citizens who do not have access to literacy and primary education attain essential information affecting their daily lives?

In the context of Nepal, one can say that the general public is at a complete disadvantage with regards to education. Nepal has one of the lowest literacy rates in the world.

The past political systems in Nepal are primarily responsible for the slow development of our education system. The Rana regime did not want the masses to get an education because they feared that an enlightened citizenry would oppose their oppressive rule. In 1853 the Rana Prime Minister Jung Bahadur, after his return from a visit to Great Britain, opened up a school for his descendants with a view to imparting English education inside the palace by bringing in British and Indian teachers. Another Rana Prime Minister, Deva Shumsher permitted selected boys from common families to attend the Durbar School. It was also during the regime of Deva Shumsher, around 1901, that vernacular schools were established and a major Sanskrit school was opened. Fifty vernacular schools inside the Kathmandu valley and 100 outside the valley were opened and teachers were appointed at a teacher-pupil ratio of 1:50. During the Prime Ministership of Chandra Shumshere, however, the 150 vernacular schools opened during Dev Shumshere's time were closed down.

To obtain government jobs during 1904-1905, a Civil Code School was established which conducted examinations known as two pass, four pass, six pass, eleven pass and fourteen pass. In 1912 the Nepali Bhasha Prakashini Samiti, a committee for publishing Nepali language books, was set up and a book on Nepali grammar called "Chandrika" was published. Despite the oppressive policy of the Rana government, in 1918 Trichandra College was founded and in 1933 the School Leaving Certificate (SLC) Examination Board was established.

As for education for girls, Padma Kanya School was started in 1947 and Padma Kanya College in 1953. In 1950 the fall of the Rana regime saw the advent of many new schools including Tribhuvan University, which was established in 1959.

After the democratic system was strangled in 1960, the tyrannical regime began to teach the lesson of "partylessness" (i.e., the one-party political system). The curricula of the country were mostly orchestrated to produce service holders rather than manpower relevant to the needs of Nepal. A country dependent upon agriculture required, and still requires, an education system that included training in the field of agriculture. Theoretical education has not been fruitful in our kind of subsistence economic system. Nepal requires professionals to be trained specifically as agricultural extension workers, health workers, veterinary workers and those who can support cottage industries.

The "New Education Plan" enforced in 1971, led to the deterioration of the standard of teaching and learning. Its educational objectives, geared toward increasing vocational skills, were limited merely to plans and were never implemented. Schools run privately by people at the local level, were taken over by the government. Schools established by the local people with people, with community cooperation, local initiative and participation, were closed down completely. The main reasons for the failure of the New Education Plan were that (1) it was imposed from above, (2) its vocational education was superficial and (3) it did not provide adequate physical

38

facilities. Again, the school committees at the local level had to face government intervention. Important school subjects such as social science and history were littered with panchayat dogma. The true facts of history were changed to flatter the royalty.

In 1981, attempts were again made to prepare curricula and textbooks in a new way, but no qualitative progress has yet been be made. Many college graduates today cannot correctly draft an application in their own language. With whom does the blame lie? With the education system or the students? Definitely, the education system is responsible for this deplorable condition.

When we look at the educational data for the past five years, on the one hand the number of primary schools has increased by about 3%, but on the other hand the overall number of students has increased by 4%. The average increase in the number of lower secondary and secondary schools is about 3% and 4% respectively, while the number of students has increased on an average about 5% and 7% respectively.

Educational Data by Level - 1989[1]

Schools	No. of Schools	Total Students	Girl Students
Primary	15,834	2,526,147	875,240
Lower Secondary	3,942	325,237	93,554
Secondary	1,791	328,779	90,792
	21,567	3,190,163	1,059,586

According to the data presented above, the attendance of girl students in primary schools is 35%, in lower secondary schools 29% and in secondary school 27%. In the same year as above, the total number of teachers was 86,397 out of which 28,577 (33%) were trained. The involvement of women teachers was 13% in primary schools, 11% in lower secondary schools and 10% in secondary schools. Overall school figures show that in the school population 33% of students are girls and 12% of teachers are women. In the SLC Examination of 1990, the number of regular students who took the exam was approximately 54,500, of which about 28,000 (51%) passed. In 1991, however, the number of those taking the exams reached 184,200, of which 48,656 (26%) passed. This was due to the changed political context, in which many schools whose recognition had

---

1 Ministry of Education, HMG, Report on Nepal's educational data, 1989.

previously been withheld, were finally recognized. In the regular SLC Examination of 1990 about 1,300 schools were included, whereas in 1991, the number of schools sending their students for the examination rose to 1,700. Naturally this large number of students who passed SLC enrolled in, and thereby placed pressure on, higher education facilities. Those who have passed the SLC Examination should be provided opportunities to obtain useful and productive employment to reduce the poverty and low economic growth which are real problems in Nepal. Otherwise all the successful SLC students will continue on to the graduate and postgraduate examinations simply because there are no alternatives. Even among the highly educated, however, only a few will get jobs, the rest will remain unemployed.

Countrywide the record of students engaged in various vocational subjects up to secondary level reveal a total of 590 students in agriculture, 725 in teaching, 482 in accounting, 69 in home science, 48 in industrial education, and 22 in religious rituals.[2] The number of girl students in technical and vocational schools is negligible.

The education of a girl is often seen is as a special favor. The illiteracy of parents, as well as social taboos and role expectations limit girls' access to education. Studies reveal that 77% of girls between 6 and 15 years old leave school. If a family suffers from economic constraints it is natural to reduce the daughter's education before the son's. Girls are involved in household work, and are invaluable since they perform almost as much work as an adult. To educate girls who are unable to attend school during the regular class time, a special teaching program of six months' duration has been organized and run by the Education Ministry in its Chelibeti (young girls) program, with a view to provide them with an equivalent of grade three education. This program, initiated about seven years ago, is being run in 64 out of the 75 districts. By 1990 the number of these schools reached 184 in all. By 1990, 3,680 girls had benefitted from these classes.[3]

A program known as "Equal Opportunity to Women in Education" was implemented with a view to raising women's awareness. The purpose of this is to train the rural women in Nepal to become teachers, and ultimately send them to teach. These female teachers are directly or indirectly playing a positive role in sending young village girls to school. There were 170 women included in the training in fiscal year 1990-1991, and 151 of them passed the examination. Twelve of them dropped out. Up to fiscal year

---

2   Ibid.
3   Neelam Basnyat, Some Insights into Female Education in Nepal, 1989.

1988-1989, about 2,350 women received training, among whom 61% now have jobs. Various literacy programs exist, yet effective implementation of these programs needs to be extended to the most remote areas.

If women working in both the formal and informal sectors were educated, it would be easier to bring about positive changes to all fields including health, environment, population, agriculture and forestry. The slogan adopted by the International Literacy Day 1991 is "Let us educate a woman: let us educate a nation." If a woman is educated, its effect is felt by the entire family and it will increase the involvement of girls in education. Despite efforts made for women's literacy in the past by both non-governmental organizations and the government programs, such as the Chelibeti program of the Ministry of Education and Culture, they were negligible in comparison to the enormity of the problem. According to WHO (World Health Organization), children of illiterate parents die in larger numbers than those of literate parents. In addition, the emphasis on women's education and literacy will make the image of women prestigious. Women would no longer be seen as helpers and housekeepers, but they would develop a sense of self-reliance with the growth of opportunities which education brings.

Besides training in knitting, sewing and home science, women's education in such areas as agriculture, health and other technical subjects where the number of girl students is comparatively low, should be encouraged. In the conditions that prevailed in the past, separate schools and colleges for girls and women were established in order to enhance women's education. There is no justification for providing education to boys and girls in separate schools. It is a good step for all schools and colleges to adopt the system of co-education.

Slogans like "education for all", or "literacy for all" do appear in the press from time to time. In 1990, the participants in the conference on "Education for All" held in Bangkok, prepared a work plan for the decade and passed a declaration that by the year 2000 A.D. all people will have an opportunity for education.

In our country today there are about 13,300,000 people over six years of age and more than 7,800,000 (59%) of them are considered to be illiterate. It is estimated that the population within this age range will reach 20,000,000 by the year 2000 A.D. Therefore, we have to think seriously about the programs related to education and literacy. The literacy rate of men as compared to women is much higher, but even so the level of male literacy is not satisfactory. From 1950 to 1992 the percentage of literate people was as follows:

Year	Male	Female	Total
1950	8.2	0.7	4.3
1960	14.6	1.6	8.9
1970	23.6	3.9	13.9
1980	34.0	12.0	24.0
1986	45.0	15.0	30.0
1990	52.0	18.0	36.0[4]

Estimate:

1992	55.0	25.0	40.0[5]

These figures may be overestimated, however, meaning that the real situation is even worse.

If women become literate, they are sure to become active participants in development activities. In training programs given by non-governmental organizations (NGO's) and the governmental agencies related to development, one of the main reason for not including women is their illiteracy. Literacy involves not only recognizing words and numbers, but also becoming socially and politically aware.

At present about 36% of the children between the ages of 6 and 10 are still not registered in school. Among the children admitted into class I, only 27% are shown to have completed education up to class V. Poverty and domestic reasons account for the 60% to 70% drop-out rate of primary school students in Asia. In Nepal the figure is as high as 73%. The nation should give top priority to children who are deprived of their basic human right to get an education. To solve this problem it is necessary to implement literacy campaigns. Despite the efforts currently conducted by the governmental agencies and NGO's, there is no effective follow-up. Thus, when the newly literate stop practicising their reading and writing skills, they again become functionally illiterate. Therefore, any temporary literacy campaign which does not have a proper follow-up program will hardly have an effect on the illiterate 64% of the population.

---

4   Ministry of Education and Culture, 1989.
5   Nepal in Figures, Central Bureau of Statistics, 1992.

An incident related to a study carried out in the district of Kabhre is quite relevant here as an example of how girls in rural areas could benefit if a follow-up program is effectively provided and pursued. Keeping in mind how she followed her mother and older sisters as their helping hand in fetching grass, firewood and water, Yangri says: "Even up to the age of ten I had no idea whatsoever that I had to study, because my two older sisters didn't go to school and my parents had no schooling of any kind; and on top of that my seniors used to tell me that in our village culture, a daughter was meant for painting the walls of somebody else's house and it was no use for her to acquire knowledge by going to school."

Five years ago, in Yangri's village of Simale, a social organization began a literacy class as an informal education program for rural women. Yangri followed her 2 older sisters who were participating in the program. Her inquisitiveness gradually evolved into an intense interest in learning to read, so she joined the class, too. She carried out her study for six months and continued with another six-month course, thus completing a full year of study.

With the skills she developed in the literacy class, this talented and hard-working girl was able to join the fifth grade at the Shri Indreshwar Primary School located in Panauti. It takes her two hours to reach the school from her village and two hours to return home. Despite continuing to cut grass for the cattle, fetching water and doing her share of household chores, she stood first in the fifth grade and completed her sixth grade standing third in the class. "Where there is a will there is a way". Even in such a situation nothing could deter her from her desire to pursue her studies. Following the example set by Yangri, four other girls from her village - Rasnali, Sita, Kamal Maya and Nangsal - attended the literacy classes and subsequently the same school in Panauti despite their similar adverse circumstances.

Yangri, now fourteen, expresses a strong desire to serve her village by becoming a medical doctor. She hopes to take care of the sick people in her rural community as a qualified medical practitioner as she has seen their terrible plight due to the lack of any modern medical facilities. Even in the midst of want and poverty and despite living a great distance from school, Yangri's sheer determination and hard work, might possibly result in her becoming a medical doctor.

Thousands of girls like her in the remote rural areas of our country are deprived of basic schooling. When will the children of our villages receive their rightful educational opportunities? In fact, it is a basic and natural right of a human being to be able to read and write, as much as to eat and to wear clothes. It is imperative that the present government with its commitment to democratic socialism, give constant attention to the education of the children of remote areas by implementing village-oriented development programs. These people deserve an equal opportunity for education which can open up many avenues for economic advancement.

- Yangri Lama on her way to school, Kavre

It is true that many more literacy programs are being implemented, but if they continue in this limited number and ineffective style, will there really be a decrease in the number of illiterate individuals? We should look at the sincere commitment of others and learn from them. For example, we find that the Kerala State of India has attained 100% literacy. Literacy programs run by the large number of Christians who live there are largely responsible for the success. In addition, the government does not interfere with religious organizations that run literacy programs.

In our "Hindu Kingdom" there is an enormous number of Hindu devotees and many offer money to the Pashupatinath temple, for example. Pashupatinath temple has its own source of income, but why does it not invest in education? Why is it unable to spend even a part of its huge resources on education? The Buddhists in some areas of Nepal have been providing education to young people. For example, a poor Sherpa family with more children than it can support will send one or more of its sons to a monastery, where he will receive not only food, but also an education.

44

The political workers of the present day multi-party system should also contribute to this field. How will false promises at election time result in real development? In many countries, the political workers, social workers and various religious people are engaged in literacy campaigns. Many schools and colleges in Gujarat and Maharashtra in India have mobilized literacy programs. The social organization of Sri Lanka named Sarvodaya has brought literacy to hundreds of thousands of people. If we were to mobilize the people of various religious abbeys, social organizations and factories in our own country, we could widen our campaign for literacy.

For concerned parents, the education of their children has become a critical problem. Most guardians have no faith in the quality of education in government schools. Privately run primary level schools have popped up on every street corner claiming to be English boarding schools, yet many of them have no proper English teachers. They keep hundreds of children crammed in small rooms, impart education by rote, the lessons of which are beyond the capacity of children's abilities and yet they charge exorbitant fees. Most schools lack even minimum facilities. There is no established standard. Privately run schools are one way to solve the problem with respect to a lack of education, but there should be a fixed government policy stating basic requirements for the establishment and running of these schools. This will be a beginning in setting and maintaining educational standards.

If the parents and guardians are worried about their children's education and future, so too must the nations think about the future of their coming generations. The European countries want to produce students capable of surviving in the new world market and the U.S.A. wants to produce students with a capacity for high-tech jobs. Japan's objective is to produce its own scientists capable of competing in the world. In Sweden there is a saying that as long as one is alive one should keep on learning. After graduation in Sweden about 70% of the students get a job within 6 months. When the education provided is not harmonious with the practical needs of a country, many economic and social problems arise. In 1991, the following countries were listed as having the top schools in the world:

New Zealand	-	Reading and Writing
Italy	-	Early Childhood Education
Netherlands	-	Language, Mathematics
U.S.A.	-	Art, Elementary School
Sweden	-	Adult Education[6]

---

6   The Ten Best Schools in the World, Newsweek, Dec. 2, 1991.

Japan and Germany spend 50% less money on each student in comparison to the U.S.A., but qualitatively they produce more skilled students. In Japan and Germany more money is spent on teachers than on students, whereas in the U.S.A. money is spent more on infrastructure.

Education should be for social change and according to the needs of one's own country. It should not be only for earning a livelihood, but for the individual's all-round development and making him or her self-reliant. The election manifesto of the Nepali Congress Party 1991, states that within the next ten years, in a program to be implemented in stages, the opportunity of elementary education will be available to all children, secondary education will be free, and within three years one more university each in both the eastern and the western regions of Nepal will be set up. Accordingly, for the academic year 1991-1992 the budget of fiscal year 1991-1992 mentions that schooling up to class six will be free.

When the new universities that have been proposed are opened, they should be polytechnic in nature. Our demand today is to concentrate on preparing skilled labor according to the needs of our mainly agriculture-based economy. "Any educational system that has no close contact with the national life is useless."[7] After secondary school level is completed there should be freedom for the students to obtain a higher education in the field of their interest. When there are no polytechnic colleges, there is no choice but to join higher education even against one's own wishes. The opportunity of higher education should be given on the basis of individual's ability and skill and those who do not qualify should be encouraged to take up job-oriented and vocational education.

Education should create inquisitiveness in an individual, make him/her think independently, develop humanitarian qualities and develop good character, self-confidence and self-reliance. When all the schools and colleges are concentrated in urban areas it is difficult for everybody to obtain an education. Again, theoretical knowledge is not enough for application in daily life. Theoretical knowledge and practical skills should go hand in hand. Although theoretical knowledge from books is the basis of education, acquiring knowledge is a never ending process. In our society, it is often felt that learning ends with the attainment of a degree. Providing the opportunity for education to girls and women and making it available to them is a serious

---

7 Bikash ke Aayam (book), Vinowa Bhave/edited by Kamala Bhasin & Abha Bhaiya, 1984.

challenge for the concerned agencies in Nepal today. Even the eighth Five-Year Plan (1992-1997) aims to make only 60% of the total population literate. To increase women's participation in getting an education, emphasis should be given to literacy classes, increasing the number of women teachers, arranging a flexible time schedule for schooling, together with long-term follow-up. Governmental and non-governmental organizations can play a vital role in increasing access to education for disadvantaged groups at the grassroots level. These programs and activities should be coordinated through the concerned authority that is represented by NGO's and government.

It is time to start thinking about making some changes in our over-all education system. All schools and colleges should be co-educational to encourage a more reasonable and healthy relationship among the students. Education at all levels, be it formal or informal should encourage critical thinking. At present there is too much emphasis on grades. Just because one can repeat a sentence or formula by heart does not mean that she/he has really understood it. Too many students graduate with good grades and little knowledge. We must make our education system more relevant and more available to everyone.

Chapter 5

WOMEN AND AIDS

The inherent power of the human body to fight various diseases is provided by the immune system. This system is destroyed by a fatal disease known as AIDS which stands for Acquired Immune Deficiency Syndrome. AIDS is caused by a virus called HIV or Human Immuno Deficiency Virus. AIDS results in a combination of infections and diseases caused by a general breakdown of the immune system in any person who is infected with HIV. The person attacked by this virus loses the power to fight infections and therefore will be unable to combat any disease so that eventually he dies. In Nepal testing for AIDS began in 1988 and so far only 114 cases (out of which 75% are female and 25% are male individuals) have been identified, but there are probably many more undiscovered. In our country it is still far from feasible for many people to have even a simple health check-up, let alone an AIDS test.

In 1985 about 2.5 million people in the world suffered from this disease. WHO (World Health Organization) has estimated that worldwide there are from 10-12 million men, women, and children who have been infected with HIV. By the end of 1991 it is estimated that the HIV virus will have infected about 20 million people, and by the year 2000 this figure could reach 30-40 million.

In 1985, 50% of all the AIDS patients were in the developing countries, whereas by 1992 this had increased to 66%. By 2000 AD, 75% of all the AIDS victims in the world will be from developing countries and by 2010 the percentage will increase and may even reach 80-90%.[1] A large portion of money to be used in the fields of educational advancement and health care will, therefore have to be diverted for the prevention of AIDS in the coming years.

---

1 AIDS in Developing Countries, World Development Report, 1991, p. 63.

According to the estimate of the World Health Organization there are 100,000-250,000 AIDS patients in India alone at the present time. This disease was first diagnosed in India in 1985, when 1 million people were tested and 5,632 were found to be HIV positive. It is known that the main carriers of AIDS in India are prostitutes and their clients, blood donors, and drug addicts. The Indian government has now taken up the case seriously in order to control this disease in an organized way.

The virus is transmitted from one person to another through sexual contact, contaminated blood and blood products, and from an infected mother to her child before or during birth. This disease can also be transmitted by unsterile needles and syringes used by AIDS patients and drug users. This disease is not communicated while shaking hands, embracing, or by casual meeting, or by the sharing of cooking pots, plates or utensils. The following types of individuals are in the high risk category for AIDS:

(a) Homosexuals
(b) Bisexuals
(c) Those who have several sexual partners
(d) Male and female prostitutes and their clients
(e) Drug addicts who share unsterile syringes

When this disease began in the USA it was found in a greater number among homosexual persons, whereas at the present time the disease has increased amongst heterosexuals, especially those who have several sexual partners. Throughout the world 60% of the AIDS patients are persons who have had heterosexual relations with many partners.

In eastern Europe, however, the virus is communicated more through sharing non-sterile medical instruments, i.e., syringes, blades, etc. AIDS can also be communicated when AIDS infected blood is transfused to another person or through the use of medicines made from infected blood. Before the fall of the Berlin Wall AIDS was said to be one of the evils of capitalism. It was claimed that AIDS did not exist in the communist countries of eastern Europe, but WHO estimates that there are more AIDS afflicted people than have been officially reported.

Throughout the world 3 million women are estimated to be suffering from this disease. In Africa 1 woman out of 40 has been found to be HIV positive. In the same manner in South America 1 out of every 500 women is infected and in North America 1 out of every 700 women is HIV positive.

The former director of the Indian Council of Medical Research, Dr. S. Pental, has said that by 1996 one woman out of every three in Bombay will be the victim of AIDS.[2] Because of this desperate situation the AIDS experts emphasize prevention by increasing people's awareness about AIDS and providing health and sex education to the community.

In Asia, however, because women are subordinate to men, and unable to insist on the use of preventive measures, they fall in the high-risk category. They are also at risk from rape. In developing countries more and more girls and women are entering into commercial sex work due in part, to the very limited economic opportunities which are open to them. And because of their low literacy level and their subordinate status they are not in a position to insist that their partners use a condom. Women have less access to information along with health care services. Women should be counseled on the risk of AIDS and how to protect their bodies. Men must also be aware of their responsibility to their families.

AIDS is prevalent and will easily become epidemic in societies where prostitution and girl and women trafficking are rampant. Out of the 2 million women involved in prostitution in Thailand, 800,000 are below 16 years of age. There is a great possibility of these girls becoming the victims of AIDS because they cannot make their male clients use condoms to protect themselves from the communication of the AIDS virus.[3] In north-eastern Thailand most women and young girls are sold into prostitution because of family poverty. When the blood of workers in 24 brothels in Thailand was examined, most of the girls carried the HIV virus.

It is estimated that there are 172,000 Nepali girls and women in the brothels of India. Rapid urbanization, extensive poverty, ignorance, and obscene films have all encouraged illicit sexual practices. Sexually transmitted diseases are therefore spreading widely, and AIDS is the most dangerous of them all. AIDS always ends in death, but not before the patient undergoes much suffering. Even before the physical symptoms begin comes the social condemnation. The person will be blamed, despised and ostracized, and as a result will become completely demoralized even before the onslaught

---

2　Dr. Mahendra Rayamajhi - How to be saved from the killing disease of AIDS?, The Gorkhapatra, November 2, 1991, (Kartik 16, 2048) and India Today, October 31, 1991.

3　The Straits Times, August 27, 1991.

of the physical suffering. So a moral dilemma arises when one finally finds out that he/she is a carrier of the disease: Should he/she reveal this fact or not? and if so, then to whom should it be revealed?

Since 1986, the central laboratory at Teku and the Blood Bank Centre at Bhrikutimandap have been doing AIDS testing, and now this testing is also done at the Teaching Hospital, Maharajgunj, Patan Hospital, the Koshi Zonal Hospital and the Western Regional Laboratory. But if few people know about AIDS, fewer still know about the test and where it can be done.

The Nepali newspapers report that health workers are terrified of the AIDS disease and are afraid to even touch AIDS patients. Some journalists have even revealed the names of those who have contracted the disease, which puts the victims in a really difficult position in society. Unless people become aware that the disease is not easily communicated, there will be panic in society.

While publishing news about the AIDS disease many factors should be considered. For example, on 28.8.2047 (Nepali date) a local newspaper reported the story about a Nepali man working for a company in Bombay for the last three years. When he returned home he donated blood to his sister-in-law who had had a serious motor accident. Since there was no time for a blood test, the brother-in-law's blood was given to her directly. Unfortunately the brother-in-law, unbeknownst to him, had the AIDS virus in his blood. Consequently, the sister-in-law got the disease through her brother-in-law's blood. When blood of the man's wife was tested it showed no HIV virus. Because of his job the man returned to Bombay, and his wife, who worked at the Gandaki Noodles factory in Pokhara, was looking after her sister who was recuperating. But as soon as the news was published about this in the newspaper with the names of all concerned, the man's wife, sister of the victim, was immediately dismissed from her job. How can this family make a living now? How can we make a place for them in our society? This is a complicated problem facing us.

In the same way a news item was published in The Rising Nepal on October 30, 1992 entitled, "Girls Back from Bombay AIDS-Afflicted". The news revealed the full names and addresses of the two victims and the fact that they had worked in the redlight district of India for 10 years. They were forced to go underground and start a new life. If they do not conceal their illness how many times must they go on moving? And if they do conceal their illness, how many others will also become victims of AIDS? In this way too, people fleeing society's rejection and condemnation will spread the disease.

Here is another news item that was published in relation to AIDS. The headline was "The Terror of AIDS in Biratnagar". The story was this: Bimala had returned from Bombay where she had worked as a prostitute. She had AIDS. When this became known, all the young men who had sexual relations with her became panic-stricken. In another case, it was suspected that five young men had contracted AIDS from Vishnu who had returned from Bombay with Bimala. Terror was spread in the region by the individuals who had enjoyed drinking and merry-making in the house of these Bombay-returned girls. The members of the gang who had taken these girls to Bombay to sell and the patients who had been injected with the same syringes used by Bimala when she was being treated for TB were placed on the list of "possible AIDS victims' by the physicians. There had been a rumor that Bimala and Vishnu were sold as early as October 1989. A group made up of Asha, alias Padma Subba, Prakash Chandhary, Raju Shahtili, Kumar Tamag, Manoj Giri, sold them to Meera Chhetri, the housemistress of Lane No. 9 in Bombay. Bimala ran away after six months, but Meera had Bimala arrested through her henchmen and sold her to Mala Lama, another housemistress. Bimala remained sick from the time she arrived there. Mala refused to treat her, but gave her Rs.500.00 and sent her back home to Nepal in April 1990. Bimala, who arrived home in the first week of April, was made to appear before the court three days after her arrival. At that time one of the civil servants had jokingly said that AIDS patients should be kept in prison, but at that time Bimala had not yet been tested so she was unaware that she had contracted AIDS. In the meantime many young men had already had sexual relations with her.[4]

Many teenagers like Bimala and Bishnu are sold, even several times and when they are no longer of any use to the brothel keepers they are returned home or just put out on the street. Once they are back in Nepal they become the butt of ridicule, mockery and laughter. Nepali teenage girls do not go to the houses of prostitution for the purpose of contracting AIDS, but unfortunately they get caught in the vicious cycle. All those who became victims of the disease because of Bimala are naturally very angry with her. Now who is to blame for these girls becoming the carriers of a killer disease?

---

4   Weekly Vimarsha, July 19, 1991.

By no means is it implied that news about AIDS should not be publicized, only that the news should be presented in such a way so as not to create a panic situation. The objective should not be to expose these AIDS victims for the purpose of causing injustice to them.

In order to cure AIDS, which is more frightening than earthquakes, storms, accidents and terrorist bombs, no injection or vaccine has yet been found. Despite billions of dollars having been spent by the American government on research only one medicine, named AZT, has been made which can only slow down the progression of the disease, but it is extremely expensive. For the people of a poor country like ours AZT is like a fruit hanging from an unreachable branch. The disease of AIDS is entering our country without any restriction. The primary source of the disease is the women returning from Indian houses of prostitution, migrant workers - Indians in Nepal and Nepalis in India - who leave their families in search of work, businessmen, and foreign tourists who visit brothels in Bangkok and Hong Kong. In all these ways the disease is making rapid inroads into Nepal.

Over the past ten years it has been noted that it is men who spread the AIDS virus much more so than do the women because men are more apt to have multiple partners, and because they are usually more mobile, thus carrying AIDS to different parts of the country and even from one country to another.

In order to prevent the spread of AIDS extensive awareness should be created among the people and general knowledge about it should be provided. The communication media and social organizations in their health care programs should include the topic of AIDS and how it can be controlled.

Because this disease can be transmitted through sexual contact, sex education is important. Both the teachers and the parents should provide proper sex education to children. It is necessary to make changes in our traditional teaching methods. To refrain from all unnatural sex relations and not to have sex with several people are examples of information which should be widely publicized.

The country's blood distribution system continues to be highly unsafe. All donated blood should be tested and care should be taken not to let AIDS pass through the medium of one patient's blood to another's.

The use of condoms is the most easily available means to save oneself as well as others from the disease. The use of condoms should be emphasized in counselling AIDS victims.

Counselling should be provided to drug addicts as well as to their families.

It is necessary to muster the active participation of the health workers, government officials and NGO personnel for the prevention of AIDS by formulating plans at the national level as well as at the district and local levels.

Chapter 6

WOMEN AND AGRICULTURE

Agriculture, the only source of livelihood for most of the people of Nepal, is not only an occupation but also a way of life. About 94% of the population of Nepal live in rural areas and earn their living from farming, whereas only 6% live in urban areas and are involved in non-farming occupations. Agriculture is the backbone of our economy. Nepali women make an important contribution to the agricultural activities of the country, but because their work is not considered productive from an economic point of view their contribution is not included in the national statistics. If women are erroneously regarded only as assistants in the agricultural field and looked upon as mere laborers, then whatever is said about having women participate in the mainstream of development will make no practical sense because they are not even credited for the major role they play.

In the prevailing situation women are involved only in the programs that are meant specifically for them. Except for plowing the fields almost every agricultural activity - like preparing the land for cultivation, carrying fertilizer, seed sowing and planting, weeding, harvesting, sorting grains, selecting and drying seeds - are particularly the responsibility of women. Almost all activities done by female peasants are labor-oriented. If opportunities were provided to them to improve their skill and natural expertise their work would be facilitated and production improved.

Two-thirds of all the farmers in our country have small plots of land where they must work hard to make their livelihood. They produce mainly rice, wheat, mustard seed and corn. A limited number of people own the majority of the farm land. Because of this unequal distribution of land, the majority of farmers are in a constant state of poverty. In our country 17% of the land is owned by 67% of small farmers who on average have farms of 1.13 hectares of land. In India the situation is similar, 25% of the land is owned by 73% small farmers who possess .65 hectare land, on average. In Indonesia 29% of the farm land is owned by 70% small farmers whose farms are .41 hectare, on average. The situation in the Philippines is almost the same as in Indonesia. Sixty percent of the farmers in Asia are small farmers and on an average they occupy between 0.3 to 1.1 hectares of farm land.[1] In Asia land ownership of the small farmers is, on an average, 1 bigha of land or about 1.5 acres.

To establish an equitable distribution of agricultural land the Land Reform Act 1964 was adopted, but because of negligence in its implementation no positive results have been seen. There was a provision for a compulsory saving scheme in the Land Reform Program in which farmers had to deposit a certain percentage of their production income - either cash or crops - and in return they would get 5% interest. They were to get back their original savings plus the interest within 5 years, but, except in only a few cases, this plan did not work out. Some members of the ward committees during that period who were responsible for implementing the savings plan embezzled the money and used the collected food-grains for their own benefit. However, because they had the blessings of the panchayat system, nobody could oppose them.

In order to bring about an improvement in the living standard of small farmers in Nepal a recommendation was made to make a survey and implement a Small Farmers Development Project (SFDP) in the decade 1970 under the joint auspices of the UN Development Program and the Food and Agriculture Organization (FAO) in the 9 countries of Asia i.e., Nepal, India, Bangladesh, Indonesia, Laos, Sri Lanka, Thailand, South Korea and the Philippines. Since 1975 the Agriculture Development Bank (ADB) with the support of the FAO has launched the SFDP in the districts of Dhanusha in the terai and Nuwakot in the mountainous region. Under the SFDP efforts are made to involve women in the programs. Women workers are posted to SFDP sites to work as motivators with rural women, and loans are floated to farmers who have organized themselves into groups. Through the extension of this program about 16,000 small farmers in all 75 districts of Nepal have received loans which to date total Rs. 1,217,118,000.00. Included in the total number of farmer groups under this program there are 2,790 women's groups.

One of the activities carried out during the Women's Decade, was a three-year study on the subject of women's status in the communities of

---

1   Dr. Bharat Prasad Dhital, Seminar paper: Women and Poverty Alleviation, 1987.

eight different ethnic groups in eight villages of Nepal, gathering data about the women's participation in and contribution to the rural economic system. According to the recommendations of that study, the Women's Development Section (under the previous Panchayat and Local Development Ministry), initiated a program called Production Credit for Rural Women (PCRW) in 1982. In this program loans are made available to rural women with the coordination of various banks on group guarantee. Up to July 1992 about 3,600 women's groups have received loans amounting to Rs. 4,57,51,152. This program gives special preference to the most remote areas of the 64 districts. Women Development offices and women workers are posted at PCRW sites to work as facilitators between the banks and rural women so that the credit component and community development activities are conducted side by side. In this way village women are developing the confidence to become involved in the programs conducted by the Women Development Division.

These two grass-root programs conducted by the government focus on small farmers and are supported by the Agricultural Development Bank and the Commercial Bank. The loans, however, are not sufficient for the small farmers and the poor classes. Those who have connections with high officials have taken advantage of the loans in the name of small farmers, whereas the banks show great reluctance to grant loans to poor rural farmers, especially women. On top of this, the process which is the same for both large and small loans, is a long and complicated one. The simplification of the loan process for small farmers has yet to be realized.

In the budget speech of the fiscal year 1991-1992 it was mentioned that in order to make loans available to the poor, a separate people-oriented agency would, if deemed necessary, be established. At the present time the following programs which target poor people and focus on small scale entrepreneurs in agriculture, cottage industry and services are related to this loan-flow:

- The Small Farmers' Development Project (SFDP)
- Integrated Banking Program (IBP)
- The Production Credit for Rural Women Program (PCRW)
- Lead Bank Scheme (LBS)
- Remote Areas Development Committee
- Cottage and Small Industries Project (CSI)

All of the above-mentioned programs are effective only in certain areas and only with accredited bank branches. It should be a priority to strengthen these programs because the infrastructure has already been set up.

The banks, however, like any business, look out for their own interests and as a result they pay little attention to smaller, less profitable loans. Consequently, the farmers are forced to follow the tradition of taking loans from merchants and traders at a high rate of interest. There are many small farmers who cultivate fields on condition that they give half of the produce to the landowner, yet even their own half they must sell in order to provide for their family's basic needs. Consequently, they must purchase most of their required staples from the merchants and traders who charge high prices.

Small farmers have to face many serious problems. There are various agricultural agencies which have been set up to help them. These agencies are located in every district, but few of the rural farmers know what kinds of services are available and how to approach them. In the agricultural branch offices there are Junior Technicians and Assistants (JT and JTA) who have to cover large areas so it is difficult for all the farmers to get their help. Also there is the Agricultural Input Corporation which is supposed to make fertilizer, seeds, and farming implements available to the farmers, but it is seldom possible to get seeds and fertilizer from them in time for planting.

Many farmers also complain that even if a loan grant is accepted from the ADB for buying a buffalo, for example, they are obligated to buy from a designated contractor. They have no choice if they want to be granted the loan. In some areas the bank personnel have accepted bribes from the contractors who want to be assured of a sale. An additional problem is that businessmen will buy up all the fertilizer and because they then monopolize the supply they can demand a high price on it and the farmers again have no choice but to pay it.

Another major concern is that if sufficient irrigation is not provided with the use of the chemical fertilizers, the fertility of the soil actually decreases over time. Therefore, the farmers who use agricultural sulphate fertilizer now have to solve the resulting problem of making the soil fertile once again.

Even after having put together everything essential for the production of food-grains, the farmer cannot sell at the most profitable price because they are exploited by the middleman. The government has so far been unable to fix prices to guarantee farmers a good return on their investment. The Nepal Food Corporation must make the necessary arrangements for the sale, distribution and storage of produce at reasonable prices. It is only when the artificial scarcity produced by traders is removed that the common people will feel secure.

To lessen and ultimately remove the deficiencies seen in the agricultural sector there should be a systemic approach to help the farmers by providing services in a coordinated way. If an arrangement could be made to provide manure, fertilizer, seeds and information from just one place, the farmers would not have to visit ten different offices. The farmers who habitually use chemical fertilizers and improved seeds will be highly discouraged if they are not made available on time. Not only this, organizations which are supposed to assist agricultural development, buy goods from traders and sell to the farmers at inflated prices.

More attention must be given to realistic irrigation projects. The agricultural sector has received more attention and investment than any of the other sectors. Large projects were conceived for the development of irrigation canals such as those of the Bagmati, Kamala, Narayani and Sunsari-Morang. The problems of large canals and dams start as soon as the natural course of the rivers is disturbed and they are forced to follow an artificial course. Such irrigation projects were more profitable for the consultants of the projects than for the farmers.

In the field of irrigation technical knowledge is essential, but so is the involvement of those who are most directly concerned, the villagers. Yet the villagers were not included in any phase of the planning or the construction. As a result, the villagers' needs were not met - and these large irrigation projects, where billions of rupees were spent, serve no practical purpose other than to pay the salaries of engineers, consultants, experts and all other support staff! In addition, there were costly technical problems. The Narayani irrigation channel, for example, has to be cleared every year because of the sand deposits which accumulate, blocking the flow of water. Constant repair and maintenance mean unending expenditures, and still the benefit to the villagers is negligible.

Only abut 18% of all agriculturally suitable land has any irrigation facility at all. Agricultural crops depend on rain. Due to environmental deterioration the problem of drought is growing. Therefore, when we see the unproductive results of large-scale irrigation projects, it is easy to see that priority should be given to smaller irrigation projects with the participation of local farmers for the benefit of local farmers. Otherwise, the irrigation activities will be limited to governmental agreements made with donor agencies and remain only in the stacks of documents while the fields of the farmers dry up.

Therefore, in our situation, giving priority to large irrigation projects has not proven to be beneficial to many farmers at all. Due to complete dependence on foreign aid, projects have been implemented not according to the needs of Nepal, but rather according to the wishes of the donor countries. As long as this attitude remains, the foreign technicians and foreign-trained experts will only go on experimenting, using our agricultural sector as their guinea pig. Only with the skill, knowledge and cooperation of the local people will the projects be both practical and sustainable.

The use of chemical fertilizers and improved seed began about three decades ago in Nepal. The proper use of irrigation, improved seed and chemical fertilizer all together, on a regular basis, and in adequate quantity, can help increase crop production for a limited time, but in the long run the fertility of the soil is actually depleted. This certainly cannot be considered to be sustainable agricultural development, rather, it is a conspiracy of multinational corporations from western countries to sell their products to the developing countries. The practice of placing ourselves at the mercy of other countries for improved seed, chemical fertilizer and agricultural lime has had an adverse effect on Nepali agriculture and has, in turn, made it entirely dependent on modern technology. With only partial information on chemical fertilizer, improved seed, and pesticides our farmers began to use them. The importance once given to cow dung and other organic manures made of decomposed materials suddenly shifted to chemical fertilizers. With the establishment of the Agricultural Inputs Corporation, the use of chemical fertilizers and improved varieties of seed was encouraged, but eyes were closed to the required irrigation facilities because the responsible western organization was only interested in making money. Because of the prevalence of such practices, the farmers, their families, and the communities of developing countries are now suffering.

According to the FAO (Food and Agriculture Organization) it is the poor nations that make the most use of chemical fertilizers. By now in our country the farmers have begun to realize the reduction of fertility of the soil due to the misuse of chemical fertilizers. In Zambia, a nation in Africa, chemical fertilizers were used blindly in the name of the Green Revolution and the result has been a substantial reduction of agricultural output. Many countries all over the world like Malawi, Hungary, Laos, and Mongolia, have begun to return to composting, using traditional manures (animal dung together with kitchen scraps and weeds). Therefore, even if improved seed and chemical fertilizers are available along with sufficient technical advice and irrigation facilities, the increased growth in production will be only temporary. To give an example, newspapers have reported that production has been doubled under the fertilizer-related input program. This program was implemented on an experimental basis in Bhiman, Panesi, Khukot, Barpalanse, Bhimeshwar, Bardeltar and Kusumtar. After a few years the farmers of those places will also put their hands on their heads, so upset will they be when they realize the negative long-term effects of fertilizer use.

Just a few years ago Nepal, which had previously been one of the major exporters of foodgrains in the world, reached a stage when it had to import foodgrains, vegetables and milk powder. This says a lot about the condition of agricultural development in this, an agricultural country. It is true that this need to import foodstuffs is partly due to an increased demand from its growing population, however, in the name of preparing the agricultural infrastructure necessary for development, most of the investment has been not for the farmers' benefit, but for the construction of impressive buildings and for other "necessities" such as motorcycles and vehicles for the staff. We have to give serious consideration once again to the projects which are adopted for implementation, that they fulfil the prerequisites of the people and are not set up just for the sake of spending foreign money.

In our country the cooperative movement began in 1956. The concept of the cooperative is that activities are performed with a collective spirit according to the wishes of its members. It was supposed to be people-oriented and based on the collective understanding of the members, be they farmers or people engaged in other occupations. In this movement, however, the cooperative committees were set up not according to the wishes of the people, but according to the recommendations of government departments and office holders. The purpose of these cooperative communities was to increase agricultural production, to help the farmers run the cooperative program in a proper way, and to make services available to the members. Committees were to be formed under the leadership of the farmers themselves. Within the cooperative framework, people would be organized according to the needs and capacities of the community. Once organized, the members were to have an opportunity to save according to their capacity and use their savings beneficially. Cooperative programs become effective only when the local groups are involved and begin to work at the very outset to fulfil their self-determined essential needs. In running cooperative programs the participation of women is essential, but ignored. The exclusion of women in these agricultural cooperative programs puts at great risk any chance of success for these programs.

Up to the present time there are about 800 cooperative organizations, both agricultural and otherwise, in the country, most of which are inactive. In some of them there is a widespread misuse of resources and in others there is a lack of resources and even the necessary operating capital is lacking. In situations where banking facilities are not available to most people, the cooperatives can help by providing loans, organizing training sessions, etc., on the basis of farmers' needs. The cooperative should be formed from within the community itself and its responsibility should be entrusted to it. The role of government officials should be limited to organizing leadership development in local people and assisting them in developing the required skills to run their cooperatives themselves.

Nowadays development workers have started talking a lot about women's participation because they have finally realized how important women's involvement is, in every aspect of daily life and therefore how essential their involvement is in all community development projects. Women are the major contributors to the family's livelihood. Eighty percent of the material needs of a household in Nepal are produced by the members of the family themselves and the major part of that is made by the women. Only 20% is bought outside the home. In this type of subsistence economy, the contribution of women is 50% of the household income, of male members 44% and of children 6%.[2] In South Asian countries the percentage of females over 10 years of age who take part in the labor force in the agricultural sector is as follows:

Nepal	96%
India	80%
Bangladesh	70%
Pakistan	60%
Sri Lanka	60%[3]

2 Status of Women, CEDA (Center for Economic Development and Administration), 1981.
3 Dr. Bharat Prasad Dhital, seminar paper: Women and Poverty Alleviation, 1987.

Statistics show that the participation of Nepali women in the agricultural sector is higher than that of women in other South Asian countries. Women form the majority of food-grain producers. Those who are most involved in the production and utilization of food-grains are definitely and indisputably the women, but when programs and/or training sessions to improve the methods of cultivation, production and harvesting are designed, no attention is given to women. Those who actually do the work are the women, but the training is given only to men. In this way our society actually discredits women's contribution, yet it is recognized all over the world that women play an extremely significant role in agriculture with their labor intensive work. There are some organizations, however, which do realize the importance of women's participation and give due emphasis to programs whose targeted groups are women.

In 1975 in the context of Women's Year, the International Labor Organization declared equal rights and equal treatment for female workers. Yet in our country there is no tradition of real ownership of land for women. If the land is in the name of a woman, it will be in name only. She cannot have ownership in a real sense. She cannot undertake any financial transaction (loans, sales, etc.) without the permission of the male members of the household.

The female headed households have to face many problems. For example, the agricultural system in Nepal depends on the exchange of labor. During the monsoon everybody is busy in cultivation all at once. After the cultivation of one family's land is finished, the land of another family is begun, using a system of exchange of labor. Plowing is a task assigned specifically to males. It is prohibited to women. Therefore, the female headed household must wait for plowing help until the work on all the other farms has been done in order to have access to male labor for plowing. It has happened that some women will plow their fields alone at night under the cover of darkness in order to advance their cultivation.

Besides the exchange of labor, other payment schemes use cash or food-grains. But for labor equal to that of the men, women will receive less - whether it be food-grains or wages. Whatever the size of the job there is discrimination against women. There is no proper assessment of the work done by women. Along with the responsibility of housekeeping and child rearing almost everything, including the agricultural work is done by women both willingly and honestly, but these laborious women are always dependent on others. To improve the living standard of the family (e.g., providing children with a variety of nutritious food and a good education), women must have access to an income. Farming is not only a means to feed the family, but if productive enough, it can be a viable source of income also.

The word "farmer" does not mean men only. Extensive training, opportunities for exchange of experiences, and visits to exhibitions should be provided to the community of farm women also. Their participation should be increased. A special preference should be given to women in the appointment of extension workers, too. If there were more women agricultural experts and workers, the women farmers could have the opportunities they need.

Until now, it can be said that the participation of women decreases in proportion to the increase of modern methods and mechanization. Therefore it is necessary to make available technical know-how and information to women farmers in order to increase production and enhance their inherent skill and income-generating ability in the agricultural field.

Chapter 7

WOMEN AND HEALTH

As the infrastructure of all human development, health is essential for everyone. It is not easy to preserve health in a developing country where the economy is in a deplorable state and at the same time, the economic and social development of a country is dependent on healthy manpower. They are interdependent elements. Fundamentally, poverty and ignorance are at the root of poor health. Almost 70% of the world's inhabitants live in developing countries, but they make use of only 17% of the entire world's income, and the lowest income of all falls to the women. The women of the world do two-thirds of the work, but earn one-tenth of the income. Most of their jobs are labor-intensive. They begin early in the morning and, in most cases, complete their work only after dark. After finishing their work in the fields they have to do the household chores. Seldom do they get sufficient calories to maintain their body in proportion to their work. In a country like ours, where there is a problem of obtaining even the minimum daily food required, the subject of health care becomes a second priority. Because of traditional concepts and social customs the health of girls and women is given little attention at all. "Throughout the developing world, more boys than girls are immunized, and girls who are brought to hospitals are generally in worse condition than boys."[1] As this social structure has so negatively affected the health and the health care of girls and women there is even a greater negative impact on everybody in the society and mainly on the children and especially on the girl child.

Most of the illnesses related to women can be prevented or cured through medical treatment, but for many reasons women are unable to take preventive measures or obtain medical treatment. Nowadays maternity-related illnesses are regarded as the most serious, although the problems of malnutrition and anaemia also take their toll on women's health. Each year 500,000 mothers throughout the world die of problems related to childbirth.

---

1 "Woman Power", Newsweek, March 9, 1992, p.26

In our country 85 out of every 1,000 women die during childbirth. Most deaths of this kind occur in developing countries, where 20% of the population is seriously effected by malnutrition, 50% do not have access to pure drinking water, and 60% do not have access to health care facilities.

Women are on society's bottom rung. Everyone prefers sons to daughters. A daughter is, after all, only something to make use of until she can be married off. It is the son who will remain at home to look after his parents in their old age, so as a result, all possible opportunities are provided to him, but not to the daughter. Daughters are compared to "banso", a common grass which grows easily. One need not care for common grass - it grows on its own, without water or fertilizer. There is no need to invest in its growth.

From the age of six, girls are expected to assist and support their mothers with the field and household chores. As wives and mothers they will be expected to do these same chores - nothing more, so no other training or education is needed.

In our subsistence economy parents regard their children as a source of labor and expect assistance from them. One of the main reasons that children are married off at a tender age is so that a daughter-in-law can be brought into the home as cheap labor. In our villages, 40% of the girls are married before they reach the age of 14.[2]   About 40% of the girls bear their first child between the ages of 15 and 19 which means that the baby will probably be of low birth weight.[3]   Childbirth before the mother is 18 years of age puts both mother and baby into a high health risk category, so for health reasons at least it is not advisable for a female to bear a child before reaching the age of eighteen. If another infant is born before the child in the lap is two years old there is a 50% possibility of the infant's death.

Most babies are born at home, with the help of midwives and/or experienced members of the household. Since the average Nepali woman gives birth to 6 children most of a women's life is spent being pregnant and taking care of suckling babies.

According to a family planning survey conducted in our country the desire to have sons by women without children was found to be 86%, and in

---

2   World Bank Report, 1989.
3   Central Bureau of Statistics, Kathmandu, Demographic Sample Survey, 1987.

68

women who have had three girls the desire for a son was 100%. Those with one son wanted another son in 90% of the cases. Nepali women bear a large number of children just because of their desire to have sons, but the number of children is determined not only by the women themselves but also according to the wishes of the family.

The main causes for the deplorable condition of women's health are social and traditional customs. In most families women eat only after everyone else has eaten. Respect for male members of the household can best be seen in the kitchen. Only in a few families do all the members of the family eat together. Usually the woman eats alone, and last of all.

The burden of work is always heavier on women. There is so much work in the fields that women are tired when they return home, but even so, they have to cook, look after their children, and see to their household responsibilities. They cannot give their full attention to nutrition, consequently the health of the whole family deteriorates.

According to a field survey done by the ILO (International Labor Organization) in Volta, a family's nutrition level was found to deteriorate in the rainy season because women had to work hard in the fields and thus had little time for meal preparation. This situation is fully applicable to our villages. From the point of view of nutrition, lentils, rice, vegetables, mashed corn, fermented greens and fermented radish, which are usually prepared in the Nepali kitchens, are highly nutritious, but the problem is that many families can neither afford a variety of rice, lentils, vegetables and mashed corn nor do they know the value of these food combinations.

Long hours are spent in physical labor by rural women involved in the agricultural sector, sowing seeds, carrying manure and fetching firewood and drinking water. During the last three months of pregnancy it is recommended that women should not do any physically strenuous work. Even so, the workload is such that if the women do not work their whole family will suffer, so dependent are they upon the woman's contribution.

There is not even minimum care for a woman either during her pregnancy or after she has given birth. She may suffer unnecessarily for hours during labor because she does not have access to hospitals or health centres or any adequate medical care. After a woman gives birth she needs rest and good nutritious food in order to regain her former health, but most Nepali women do not even get to rest for more than a few days, and as a result, many health problems occur. One of the most frequent health problems of these women is prolapse of the uterus. Another serious postpartum condition is vesica-vaginal fistula, the rupture of the urinal bladder with parts of their inner organs coming out of their vaginas. In order to cure vesica-vaginal fistula, a major operation is required which takes at least 5 hours. Until recently, Dr. Sylvia Scholz, a German gynecologist working at Patan Hospital, was doing this operation with much success. The women who suffer from this condition are shunned even by their own families because their urine cannot be controlled so they have an unpleasant body odor and, in addition, it is not possible for them to have sexual relations. Their life is full of pain and suffering. It is easier for the husband to get another wife than to find the money necessary to cure his own wife, so no attention is given towards her treatment. Such women are usually abandoned. Due to this extreme discrimination by the family, these women can become mentally disturbed as well.

Without basic medical treatment ordinary diseases can become serious ones - limbs are lost and lives are lost. Because of the discrimination in getting adequate medical care for women, women's life expectancy in Nepal is only 51.37 years, while that of men is 54.98 years, in contrast to the situation in more developed countries where women's life expectancy surpasses that of men's.

In our country the majority of people live in rural areas. It is difficult for these people to benefit from the various types of information and services which are available in the urban areas, and few, even among the educated youth, have a good understanding of the structure and functioning of the human body. There is a lack of knowledge even of basic first aid amongst the majority of people in the rural communities who do not have even a minimal education. A basic knowledge of health care is extremely necessary for women, but men too should be made aware of all aspects of basic health care. As it stands now, women assume full responsibility for all aspects of primary health care like health education, prevention of communicable diseases, family planning and mother and childcare, immunizations, treatment of common diseases, nutrition, and hygiene. Women have been fulfilling this responsibility by learning from the experiences of their own mothers and grandmothers, but both men and women should be responsible for looking after the family, obtaining information about the importance of health care and putting the knowledge thus gained into practice.

The job of giving birth belongs to a woman, but many members of the family are involved in raising the child. Therefore, in order to bring about a positive change in many traditional concepts towards health care it is not enough to provide information to women only. Only when all the members of the family are aware can a real change in attitude be brought about in matters of health care. It requires everybody's participation.

It has been established that for a child no other food can compare in nutritional quality with mother's milk. Mothers working in urban areas have a greater pressure to feed powdered milk to their children than the women in rural communities. Few urban mothers breasteed either because of the influence of powdered milk advertisements or because they must work outside the home. The majority of rural women with or without the knowledge of the importance of mother's milk give it to their babies automatically, but because these breastfeeding mothers do not get adequate nutritious food they start to give solid food to their babies at an early age. Babies fed on mother's milk can be safe from diarrhoea, colds, influenza and other such diseases.

The village people have their own unique concepts of human anatomy. For example, if asked to describe sterilization of a woman, the villagers say that the uterus has been turned upside down. Whatever means of family planning may be adopted, it is necessary to have an idea as to what its effects are on one's own body. It is necessary for women to know about the structure of their body and how it functions.

The traditional concepts of menstruation have a negative effect on the health of girls and women. Most girls begin menstruating between the ages of 11 and 16. A girl should be told about menstruation before it actually happens by her mother, older sisters or senior female members of the family whose responsibility is not only to teach household chores, but also to educate about the sexual functioning of her body. When open and frank exchanges of views and advice with superiors are lacking the girls will develop their own ideas from conversations with their peers. If education abut sex is not provided to both the boys and the girls by responsible adults, their inquisitiveness will be limited to asking their friends. In this way they do not always get proper information and may form many wrong concepts. During the period when a girl begins to menstruate the family should create a positive environment of support and information in order to increase the girl's self-confidence. She should be made to feel that this is just a natural function of her body and certainly nothing of which to be ashamed.

In a woman's life illnesses specific to females are not limited to pregnancy and childbirth. Health care services and information should not be limited to the time of child bearing and child rearing. Women spend most of their time caring for others, whether it be children or other members of the family as mothers, mothers-in-law, daughters-in-law, or grandmothers. Many women during menopause remain in tension and despair without understanding where these feelings come from.

In old age both men and women suffer from a lack of good health care. When giving emphasis to primary health care, it is advisable to pay attention also to the problems and needs of the elderly. Too often old people are ignored and their illnesses neglected. Families living in poverty do not have the means to invest in their elder members.

Grandmother taking a rest from carrying a load typical Nepali style, Kavre

The importance of food comes as a first priority for health and bodily development. Many diseases are caused by the lack of necessary nutrients, vitamins etc. in the body, and even when nutritious food is available people can lead a sickly life not knowing how to eat nutritiously. Junk foods like ready made biscuits, noddles, cheeseballs, are easily available and very popular in both the towns and the villages. Many of these products contain ajino moto (monosodium glutamate or msg) which can cause brain damage in children under 6 years of age, according to the recent findings of scientists. In some developed countries foods containing msg (ajino moto) are banned. In India consumers' committees have begun campaigns to make the people aware of the ingredients in the foods they are eating. In this regard the label for instant bouillon cubes contains a warning that the product contains msg and therefore should not be given to children. Nepal has yet to take such action. In some food items various color additives are used which may be dangerous to health, but we are eating them anyway. Only when consumer groups become active in Nepal will we really be able to find out what we are actually eating in these processed foods.

Superstition is often linked to the traditional treatment of illness. For example, emaciation is a condition in children caused by malnutrition. A malnourished child needs food frequently throughout the day, but traditionally such children are often taken to temples of gods and goddesses because the disease is interpreted as "an attack of spirits". Smallpox, too, used to be considered a curse from the Mother Goddess, but with the eradication of smallpox by vaccine, such a belief has been discouraged to a great extent.

In the poor economic conditions like ours in rural Nepal and because of the lack of physicians and hospitals, junior health workers could play a more significant role. In addition, the traditional healers like shamans and midwives, who are still held in high esteem in rural communities, have, in many areas, already been drawn into the primary health care system, and their participation should be encouraged. These traditional healers usually dispense the locally available herbs which are effective and safe, but many have now started using modern medicines also. This traditional aspect of using natural herbal medicines should be encouraged because these resources are readily available right in the village. Some diseases can be cured by domestic treatments, whereas some others can easily be cured by modern medicines. Therefore, if the health care services presently existing in urban areas were also made available to the rural communities, the role of the primary health care centre would be given the importance it deserves. Instead of trying to install health care facilities all over the country all at once, we should pay more attention to preventive health care services by providing adequate training to the traditional healers.

Altogether 134 nations, including Nepal, took part in a conference on Primary Health Care held in Alma Ata in the former Soviet Union on September 12, 1978. It was decided there that any nation making a plan of health care and implementing it should give priority to people's participation. Unfortunately even up to now there is still no provision for primary health care for everyone in our country.

73

Women could use their own knowledge and skill (as passed on from their mothers) if only they had more self-confidence and accurate information. This could be enhanced through training courses in basic first-aid, nutrition and health care.

In the past, nursing and health services were considered as belonging exclusively to women, but in the last few years men have also begun to take up nursing training. Even if there is a special significance of women in the community, we should encourage the participation of men also in family health care. At a time when the killer disease AIDS is spreading so rapidly not only the adult men and women but also the youth should be included in the community health care programs.

Chapter 8

WOMEN AND THE MEDIA

Communication is the exchange of information. Words are not always needed - intention may be understood through gestures and non-verbal expressions. Thus communication can take place in various ways. The main media of communication today are radio, television, telephone, films, plays, newspapers, posters, photos, songs, dialogues, speeches, etc. Nowadays the media can spread messages and information about a variety of activities quickly and easily from one place to the other thus ensuring a well-informed and aware society. The role of the media should be to inform in order to bring about positive changes in society.

The active participation of women began to be considered indispensable in developing countries in every aspect of life, including economic, social and political within the last ten or fifteen years. It is relevant to discuss the role of the media in making all people aware of the significance of women's contribution to society. How have the media targeted women? How have they portrayed women? What is their effect on women? And, more specifically, how much attention is given to rural women? In other words, how effective is the communication sector in projecting present day social realities? Does it have a commitment to portray women's contribution in a positive light? It is necessary to examine these questions.

First of all we have to remember that 60% of the women in the world are illiterate, and that this percentage is even higher in developing countries. Therefore, few women can be reached through printed materials such as newspapers, books and journals.

Educational materials, books relating to job-oriented adult education, children's books, programs published on development, etc., mostly uphold the traditional role of women with no reference to the role of today's professional and working women. With a view to changing this situation, the world conference held in Nairobi in 1985 in relation to the Women's

Decade published the Forward Looking Strategies for the Advancement of Women in the form of recommendations and conclusions. One of their conclusions was that there will be no change in the social attitudes and concepts regarding women as long as women are reflected as sex objects or traditional housewives by the advertising agencies and the communication media.

In order to bring about an attitudinal change in the people regarding women and their role in society, there needs to be an increase in the active participation of enlightened women in the communication sector itself. For this to happen, conducive policies should be formulated. The representatives of 157 nations, including Nepal, indicated their agreement to this at the Nairobi conference.

According to a research report on women in the media, women represent fewer than 30% of the employees in the national newspapers and magazines, films and in radio broadcasting in most countries of the world. Furthermore fewer than 10% are engaged at the management level.

The main reasons for the limited involvement of women in the press and in the field of writing are that they are deprived of educational training opportunities. They are kept isolated from the acquaintance and exchange of ideas with the outside world, and they are burdened with household chores. Even if a woman has sufficient talent, it is difficult for her to come out as a writer. This fact is made clear by the experience of some famous women writers. In America, writing took second place for Harriet Beecher Stowe who wrote <u>Uncle Tom's Cabin</u>, a book which helped to mobilize support for the abolition of slavery. Her first priority was to be a wife and mother, and she had difficulty in finding a peaceful corner of the house where she could write.

Elizabeth Cady Stanton, that great fighter for women's rights in America, especially suffrage, could never have written her most famous speeches and articles if her dear friend and fellow warrior, Susan B. Anthony (who never married) had not come to her home and looked after her seven children so she could have the peace to write.

Nadine Gordimer, who received the Noble Prize for Literature in 1991, is a South African writer whose fight against apartheid is reflected in her short stories and novels. It cannot have been easy for a white woman to hold such views.

Parijat, a popular writer of Nepal, who passed away on April 15, 1993, was a feminist who contributed a lot to Nepali literature. Her short stories, novels, poems and essays uphold and further the cause of women. She was wholeheartedly engrossed in studies and writing and had said that she wanted to breathe her last while engaged in writing.

Shashi Kala Sharma edited the important journal Swasnimanchhe (Women) between the years 1958 and 1968. Not only was she a rare female journalist at that time, but she edited the first and, for several years, the only women's magazine.

Maya Thakuri and Bhagirathi Shrestha have, for many years, been writing short stories about the many aspects of women in our society. Although it is true that even male writers in our society are rarely able to devote themselves solely to writing, because they must work at other jobs, at least men do not have to see to the feeding of children and household chores as well.

Nowadays many women have been contributing articles to periodicals and newspapers on women's issues. There are four magazines at present devoted solely to women's issues: Asmita, Nari Manch, Richa and Riwaj. Their offices are located in Kathmandu, but the circulation is countrywide.

The media programs for women are still based on the image of women as "ideal" (docile) housewives. This image persists in information on family planning and mother and child care also, as given by radio, television, newspapers, magazines and even school books. For decades now the Women's Program run by Radio Nepal has provided women only with recipes and beauty tips, whereas our need today is to give practical and relevant information of and about women. To give information on how to cook halwa, puri and achar (pickles), how to color one's hair, and how to apply lemon face masks, as is done by Radio Nepal, is a gross misuse of valuable media time and money and an insult to women's intellect.

Many songs broadcast through Radio Nepal are demeaning to women. For example, many popular songs express the ideas that women are not worthy of friendship, are always crying bitterly, and are happy only when they have a new sari and bangles.

The great poet Bhupi Sherchan is honest about the real situation of women as can be seen in the following lines:

Enclosed within four walls
Is a cupboard
And within it
Four saris.
Woman! That's it:
Your life's acquisition!

Of course this situation developed through a long course of history, and only in the last few years have women been able to break out of their four walls.

The attitude of the famous playwright Bal Krishna Sama towards women shows the importance of a co-existence of the sexes:

"Woman gives birth to man;
Man is her co-traveller"

Our communication media today do not pay any attention at all to the concept of coexistence between men and women. The popular media like radio and television, together with the textbooks used in schools and informal education classes, etc., portray Nepali women as persons useful only for household chores and as mothers and housewives. In reality however, in our kind of subsistence economy, statistics confirm that rural women contribute more to food production than do men, but their contribution is never acknowledged.

In most of the publicity for consumer goods women are exhibited in advertisements for toothpaste, bath soap, washing soap and food items and from pots and pans to wall hanging calendars. The women are certainly not presented in a way that ordinary women can relate to. For the purpose of attracting the attention of the audience, women are used in advertisements as well-dressed or half-dressed decorations. We see women in fancy saris washing their husband's and children's clothes to the tune of musical instruments. Neither do these women in the ads look tired nor does it look like they are working very hard. What do ordinary women feel about these ads and how do they compare them with their actual life? It must be like a fairy tale.

Our young people are being encouraged to smoke a particular cigarette, drink a particular beer. Misleading publicity is widespread, such as cigarette ads that show how a person becomes manly by smoking. The man is capable of rescuing someone who is about to fall through a dilapidated bridge or he achieves skill overnight to be able to hit the bull's eye, inferring, of course, that these feats were all attained by smoking this or that cigarette! Our chief communication media like the radio, television, newspapers and magazines have also begun to give much publicity for cigarettes and intoxicating drinks. Such socially harmful publicity should be stopped immediately.

Some changes have already taken place. Radio Nepal's newstime used to be Star Beer Time, and Nepal television's newstime used to be San Miguel (a local beer) Time. Instead, now our news program are sponsored by the tea companies.

The communication media has had a major influence in making liquor and cigarettes acceptable and even desirable as if they were essential, basic needs of the people from the hills to the terai. In a country like ours where most of the population is surviving from hand-to-mouth, the role of the mass communication media is indeed very important. In a country which has one of the lowest literacy rates in the world, the information given through the media can have an indelible effect. Can we create tomorrow's moral and prestigious society by remaining silent observers of these misleading commercial ads?

The practice of presenting women in the media as recreational sex objects, brainless, helpless, weak and snivelling as an attraction for the sale of commodities should be abandoned without delay. The rural women, who fulfil the role of active participants in our country's economic upliftment, should be made aware of their inherent power and ability, and the communication media should produce programs to this effect. The mass media are meant not only for urban dwellers; they should inspire and encourage rural people towards real development.

The women themselves are accountable for highlighting their contributions and enhancing their prestigious image. In order to bring about a change in the concept of women's image it is necessary for them to be qualified in professional skills rather than to take part in dress competitions through the powerful mass media. The living picture of women engaged in every field should be presented.

It must be said that Radio Nepal has also been running some informative women-targeted programs. One is "Chelibeti" which focuses on girl and women trafficking. The other is the "Rural Women's Program", which is written and paid for by the Women's Development Division of the Ministry of Local Development. Other programs, too, although not women-specific, are presented, but most if not all, are paid for by the particular organisation. Nowadays there are alot of like-minded NGO's that are eager to speak out about pressing issues that must be addressed, but the main daily newspapers (Rising Nepal and Gorkha Patra) as well as Nepal T.V. and Radio Nepal are all government owned, making the programs too costly and controlled. If these like-minded NGO's could come together to establish their own radio and T.V. stations, we would be able to see a great change in the level of awareness of our society. For example, programs for farmers will not have to show old, experienced women farmers listening passively to a lecture by a junior technical assistant as if she knows nothing at all about farming. And programs can show the changing roles of women and men where women are entering public life and men are helping around the house.

Furthermore, radio and T.V. programs, free from government control, will be able to address sensitive issues on the environment, prostitution, AIDS, child labor, to name only a few, in an open, spontaneous, and honest way.

Chapter 9

WOMEN AND DEVELOPMENT

The definition of a plan is: a proposed method by which a definite purpose can be achieved. In order to fulfil the purposes laid down in development plans, various courses of action are adopted, which are known as policy. In our country, planned development started thirty-five years ago, and although seven five-year plans have been implemented, the very minimum needs of the common people have not yet been fulfilled. Although the majority of the people live in rural areas and 94% of them are engaged in agriculture, the programs based on the plans did not reach them. The problem of poverty has been a formidable challenge, with the chasm between the rich and the poor growing every day. Some of the major indicators of a country's level of development are: the ability of the people to feed themselves adequately (at least two well-rounded meals a day), favorable conditions in which to bring up children, the accessibility of health care facilities and the level of education available.

In the first five time-bound plans there was no mention of women's participation. In reference to International Women's Year, 1975, the World Women's Conference held in Mexico City had decided that every nation should implement its women development projects on the basis of the necessity and demand of the country after preparing a national activity-plan through governmental and non-governmental agencies. In this connection, the Sixth Five-Year Plan (1980-1985) stated: "With a view to involving women in the country's all-round development it is most necessary to mobilize women's participation today in the developmental process because there is a greater significance of women in economic, social, political, religious, cultural and all other fields."[1] As a result, institutions related to women were established at the governmental level and some organizations

---

1   Sixth Five-Year Plan (1980-1985), The Policy of Increasing Women's Participation in Development Activities, p. 212.

were set up also in non-governmental fields in order to encourage women to assume an active role in community development.

In the same way, the Seventh Five-Year Plan (1985-1990) had adopted a national policy in relation to women's participation with the statement: "Women comprise 48.8% of Nepal's total population and form a potential work force of the nation. It is self-evident that if this productive force is mobilized the development rate can be raised higher with a steady growth of production. It is, therefore, extremely necessary to create a proper atmosphere and adequate opportunities for women to participate in the process of country's development on a equal footing with men."[2]

In accordance with the recommendations made by the above-mentioned International Conference in Mexico in 1975 His Majesty's Government (HMG) prepared a national work-plan for women's development based on suggestions from various governmental agencies and NGO's. It set up the Women's Services Coordination Committee (WSCC) which was responsible for coordinating the activities around this work-plan. The objective was to mobilize women and increase their participation in six different areas: agriculture, education, employment, health, law, and cooperatives. In the sixth and seventh plan periods, a separate chapter on policies for women's development was included on the basis of this work plan. This work plan emphasized the reservation, or quota system, to ensure the participation of girls and women in each of the areas mentioned above. Its policy was to make the necessary amendments to laws that obstructed women's development. Even though the objectives were fixed through the coordination of all the concerned agencies and institutions, the implementation of these objectives was negligible.

The Seventh Plan (1985-1990) stated the necessity of properly evaluating the economically active women workforce. The following objectives were set after accepting the necessity of extending the limited opportunities of female participation in the decision-making process of various levels:

---

2   Seventh Five-Year Plan (1985-1990), Women's Participation in Development Activities.

Objectives

1. For the development of women, who exist as a great labor force, suitable opportunities should be provided and in every aspect of the country's development they should be enabled to mobilize themselves for their active participation.

2. For the all-round development of women their economic and social status should be raised.

3. The talents and skills that women possess should be respected and they should be developed as capable and productive citizens for gradually making them self-reliant.

For achieving these objectives women were supposed to be given increased access to education, health and agriculture facilities, as well as an increase in employment opportunities. They were to be included in health education activities and priorities were also to be given in agricultural training activities. In the same way it was envisaged in the policy that women be included in all fields of forestry and cooperatives, but in practice these objectives and policies proved overambitious and remained only on paper. How can the desires, expectations and necessities of people be fulfilled by plans that are impractical and whose implementation aspect is weak? If only one-fourth of the objectives had been fulfilled, a great improvement in women's condition would have been seen by now. The huge gap between saying and doing naturally resulted in the people's indifference to the ineffectual programs. Almost all development organizations and institutions have a women's component, but in most cases only a token woman is included in an effort to show that their program encourages women's participation.

Only one new provision has been included in the approach paper of the Eighth Plan (1992-1997), item (g.) which refers to revising laws discriminatory to women. The strategies listed in the Plan which are to be followed are:

   a. Encouraging women's participation in traditional as well as in non-traditional sectors.
   b. Extending access to formal and non-formal education to women.
   c. Adopting affirmative action in hiring and training programs.

d.   Increasing women's access to health facilities, especially family planning and maternal/child health facilities.
e.   Increasing women's access to credit, technical knowledge, entrepreneurship development programs, marketing facilities and employment opportunities.
f.   Extending to rural areas those kinds of technological changes which reduce the time spent in gathering and fetching fuel, fodder, water, and in household work.
g.   Revising laws discriminatory to women.

None of the objectives were ever fully met, yet still they were increased in the following plan periods. It is appropriate to present a small example to prove that the plans to be formulated in the coming years should not be over-ambitious, but made only after a thorough review and evaluation of the previous plans.

In the Fourth Five-Year Plan (1970-1975) a target was set for making 100,000 people literate. In the same way, in the Fifth Five-Year Plan (1975-1980), 600,000 people were targeted for literacy, and this figure increased and reached 900,000 in the Sixth Five-Year Plan (1980-1985). But in the beginning years of the Sixth Five-Year Plan, the statistics show that altogether only 272,000 were made literate. Thus in the decade 1970-1980, only negligible work was done to increase the literacy rate in proportion to the highly inflated objectives. Again in the Seventh Plan (1985-1990) a target was set to make 1.5 million people literate, whereas only 0.97% of the total budget was allocated for informal education in fiscal year 1983-1984. In fiscal year 1984-1985 this amount was decreased to 0.83% and fiscal year 1985-1986 allocated just 0.29% of the total budget.[3] In the same periods as the targeted number of people went on increasing the budget allocation was decreasing.

An equitable distribution of means is essential in order to assist the people in developing plans which will bring about an improvement in their standard of living. If people could be raised above their poverty, disease, hunger and ignorance, the development efforts would be meaningful. Among the rural communities half of the population are women. Women must have informal education and training so that they can be involved in the village development activities. Providing education on a discriminatory basis

---

3   Children and Women of Nepal, UNICEF, 1987, p. 140.

according to sex will hamper the development of not only the village, but also the whole country. Only when women's participation is increased at the village level will the common women benefit.

- *The author with village women in group discussion, Kavre*

The plans at the national level have not recognized the real contribution of women. The national census does not even collect data about the work performed by women in their domestic life in a subsistence economy. Most of their contributions go unnoticed. Therefore, a study was carried out to determine the actual situation of women. On the basis of the findings of "The Status of Women",[1] organizations began to target women for specific programs for their upliftment. How can the living standard of the population be raised without developing the human resources and work force which form half the population of the country and without assessing the contributions they make to national production?

Only those programs targeted specifically for women have been able to mobilize female participation to any extent. Even if a women wants to go into business, it is beyond her reach to get a loan from the bank because she has no access to collateral. Neither does a social atmosphere exist which might facilitate and encourage the loan application process for her because of the prejudice against women nor does she have any established economic

---

[1] The Status of Women, Center for Economic Development and Administration (CEDA), 1981.

rights. Even in programs to start small-scale industries where loans are available exclusively for women without collateral, the bank staff are uncooperative and make it difficult for the women because of the small amount of the loans. In order to make government services available for women, (the services of which are readily available to men), the concerned development worker must convince those in charge that women should also be able to avail themselves of such services.

The planners should give priority to the basic needs of the people. Women, who make up half of our society, must be included in all projects and their productive skills increased. All forms of gender discrimination must be completely eliminated. In fact, in our rural communities where all family members have to live under the yoke of poverty and want, gender discrimination will only increase their poverty.

The previous plans could not be implemented because of the inability to recognize the needs of the people and the lack of people's participation themselves in fixing the target. Furthermore, the policies and goals were unrealistic because the government lacked the resources to carry them out. More important, however, was the lack of political stability and of commitment on the part of those responsible for the implementation of the plans. Government efforts, in any case, are not enough. NGO's must also contribute so that women's real participation will result in real progress. In a situation where development has become a national challenge, the people themselves (especially women) must be involved in the complete process, from the planning through the implementing stages, so that real development can take place.

Chapter 10

WOMEN AND CHILDREN

Nepal's future rests on the shoulders of its children. Of our country's total population, 40% are children below 15 years of age. According to existing laws, children are defined as those who are below 14 years of age. Most of the children of Nepal are deprived of any opportunity to learn to read and write, to eat until their stomachs are full, to wear adequate clothing - that is to say, they do not have even the minimum necessities of life. Are there any parents who have no desire to see their babies healthy, well-fed, educated and industrious? But most of the families work for low wages on landowners' fields or on their own tiny plots of land for their livelihood. It is difficult for them to even collect food grains sufficient for the whole year.

These subsistence farmers rely on the help of their children. In fact, from about the age of six the children begin to assist their parents in their work. Of all the children, about 60% are engaged as field laborers. Thousands are obliged to work as bonded laborers.

Children from rural and semi-rural areas who come to towns in search of work are usually employed as domestic servants, cooks and dishwashers in restaurants and hotels, brick makers, carpet weavers, porters in bus stations, boot polishers, newspaper vendors, etc. And some of them make their living by garbage picking and begging, too. Hundreds of children spend their lives on the streets and lanes of Kathmandu. If the nation does not pay attention to the plight of the street children immediately, these vulnerable children may never be able to play their rightful role as responsible citizens of our country. Urgent attention must also be given to the problem of trafficking. Innumerable girls have been sold for prostitution both inside and outside the country. In rural, semi-rural and even in urban areas children are being exploited in various ways and are victims of injustice.

The present condition of the children of Nepal is closely associated with the economic, social, political and cultural condition of the country. Every child who is brought up in the lap of want and poverty in developing countries is burdened with responsibilities equal to those of an adult, and all this even before he or she has had the chance to finish his/her physical development. They are forced to grow up before their time. In the same way, they also age more quickly.

Being unable to pay the loans borrowed for the family's survival, the parents are forced to "sell" their children to work as bonded laborers. In Nepal, India, Pakistan and Bangladesh there is a major problem of bonded child labor. It is estimated that the number of child laborers in Asia is about 261,300,000.[1] In America also a significant number of children are in dire straits. About 500,000 to 700,000 children in the USA are homeless and about 10,000,000 are suffering from the scourge of poverty.

In Nepal the chance of a new born baby's survival is only 50%. Before reaching the age of one year, one child out of ten dies in Nepal, whereas in a developed country the mortality rate is one child in every forty. In developing countries the mortality rate of girls is higher than that of boys. In the decade of 1971-1981 the mortality rate of male children in our country per thousand was 144.5, whereas the mortality rate of female children per thousand was 150.38.[2] According to a study made in India the death rate for girls below 5 years of age is 23%, whereas the death rate for boys is 19%. In the same way, for Bangladesh children between 1 and 4 years of age the death rate of girls is 46 percent higher than that of boys.[3] In India the ratio of males to females is one thousand males to 935 females (1000 : 935). According to the census taken in Nepal in 1981 the male/female ratio was one hundred five men per one hundred women (105 : 100), whereas the preliminary results of the 1991 census show that there are 99.78 males for every hundred females. (99.78 : 100). In South Asia as a whole the number of women is fewer than the number of men. At the present time Nepal is the only exception. The veracity of the statistics can be a topic of debate.

The main reasons for child mortality are malnutrition, diarrhoea, measles, whooping cough, tetanus, diphtheria, tuberculosis, pneumonia and typhoid. Oral medicine is given to babies to save them from the crippling disease of polio. Among the diseases just mentioned, some can be cured and many are preventable through vaccines. About 3.5 million children die every year from diarrhoea in the world because of the dehydration it causes. The oral use of the mixture of salt, sugar and water has begun to save millions of children worldwide from death from dehydration. In our country 43,000 infants die annually from diarrhoea. According to UNICEF and WHO (the World Health Organization) the most successful health care achievement in

---

1   Bal Sarokar, CWIN, Year 1, Issue 1, p.15.
2   Dr. Suvarna Laxmi Singh, Overview of the Girl Child in Nepal, UNICEF, 1989.
3   Facts for Life, UNICEF, WHO, UNESCO.

the 1980's was that 80% of the infants below one year of age in the world were vaccinated against disease, but as far as the developing countries were concerned, only an average of 50% of the infants were immunized against disease.

Poverty and difficult economic circumstances affect children and their families all over the world. Even in an affluent country like the USA, there are 5.5 million children below 12 years of age who are suffering from malnutrition. In various countries the number of malnourished infants are as follows: [4]

Country	Number of malnourished infants
China	24 million
South Asia	76 million
Other countries in Asia	39 million
Africa	300 million
America	8 million

Due to a shortage in the food supply after the Gulf War a vast number of the 3.5 million children in Iraq suffered from malnutrition and infectious diseases. Besides these children, there are many other children who have also suffered the ravages of war. Up until 1945 those who suffered the ravages of war were mainly soldiers. In the 150 wars fought in the world since then, about 20 million people have died and 60 million have been injured. Most of the dead and injured were civilians, and among the civilians naturally were many women and children. Children in unknown numbers were killed, orphaned or left homeless. Today about 7 million children in Africa live in refugee camps. Because of wars schools and health clinics are closed and food stocks are destroyed. At the present time, even the children under 15 are employed by the millions to fight in the war.

According to a study conducted by UNICEF in connection with the SAARC Year of the Girl in India, 25% of Indian girls die before they reach 15 years of age. There is also a growing tendency to destroy females before they are born. Parents are now able to determine the sex of the foetus by ultrasound and by amniocentesis. In 1990 among the 8,000 foetuses destroyed through abortion in 6 hospitals of Bombay, 7,999 were female.[5] In those areas where the dowry system is entrenched, abortions of female foetuses are more prevalent.[6] In Maharashtra, a province in India,

---

4 The State of the World's Children, UNICEF, 1990.
5 "Women Power", Newsweek, March 9, 1992, p. 26.
6 Women's International Network News. 1991.

amniocentesis has been prohibited. Attempts have been made to ban it nationally, but without success.

A strong suspicion cropped up after the results of the census in China in 1990 which made public the fact that 5% of girl infants were "lost" after birth. Nothing is clear about the loss of these infant girls. According to researchers among those lost, some are being brought up secretly, some are kept with relatives, but most of them are murdered. About ten years ago in China the policy of bearing only one child per family was strictly enforced. Parents wishing a son would either murder a girl child or bring her up secretly. Those whose first child happened to be male had themselves sterilized, but for those whose first child was a girl, the only way for them to have a son was either to hide the girl infant or to murder her. In 1990 alone, about 600,000 girl infants were "lost". According to the 1990 census, for every 100 girls under the age of one year there were 111.3 boys in the same age group (100 : 111.3); whereas in 1987, the ratio of girls to boys was 100 : 110.5. In 1964, for every 100 girl infants there were 105 boy infants (100 : 105).[7] By now this sex ratio has changed to give way to a different situation. The main reason for fewer girl infants is that they are killed before birth. Although in China since 1987 laws have forbidden the physicians to reveal the sex of the foetus when discovered by ultrasound tests, in practice live girl births keep on decreasing.

When we look at the number of Nepali children under 15 there are fewer girls than boys. Abortion is not legal here, yet it is performed in private clinics. The practice of finding out the sex of the foetus through the ultrasound test and performing an abortion if the foetus is female has not come into effect; we have not heard of it in Nepal as yet. But the daughter is not treated in the same way as the son from birth. Little attention is given to a daughter in matters of nursing, feeding and medical care. Due to this discrimination the mortality rate of girl infants has been much higher than that of boys.[8]

Child Population According to Sex

Year	Total Child Population	Boys	Girls
1971	4,674,578	2,379,422	2,295,156
	(100.0)	(50.91)	(49.11)
1981	6,211,972	3,227,012	2,984,900
	(100.0)	(51.91)	(48.01)
1988	7,962,450	4,159,359	3,803,091
	(100.0)	(52.24)	(47.76)

7   Women's International Network News, 1991.
8   Central Bureau of Statistics, Population Census, 1981.

90

The table above clearly shows that the number of girls under 15 years of age in comparison to the number of boys is decreasing, although according to biology, girls are physiologically stronger than boys.

Obstacles to Child Welfare

In our society the parents bringing up their children can themselves be deprived of the basic necessities of life. The parents too can be victims of poverty. There may be a lack of successful methods in using the goods they possess. Oftentimes the means of production are owned by a limited number of individuals. Somehow or other the problem of obtaining two meals a day preoccupies them most. An illustration of such abject poverty can be found in the practice of some families who have many children (7 or so) where a tika (a red mark) is place on the forehead to indicate which child has eaten and to prevent him/her from having a second helping because there is not enough food and it must be rationed.

The mortality rate is higher in rural areas where the death of children is a regular occurrence. In the villages, especially in poor families, the death of domestic animals and cattle is a more serious matter than that of children. It can easily be understood, then, how terrible is the condition of the poverty in our country when one is more saddened at the death of an animal than of a child. The village children who do have an opportunity to study must cut grass, fetch firewood and drinking water before going to school. And besides all this work, the girls also have to do the household chores and tend to the younger children, so they have to work harder than boys and do more to help their mothers. Girls of rural communities between the ages 10 and 14 work on average 7.31 hours a day while boys of the same age group work only 4.5 hours.

Although the children of educated parents in urban areas, as compared to those children in rural areas, do not have to bear as much physical labor, they do have more mental pressure. Most parents regard their children as reflections of themselves and feel that society will judge them by the success or failure of their children, so it is only natural that they expect much from them. Too many parents expect their children to fulfil their own unfulfilled ambitions. But in the real world there is no guarantee that children, even with all the educational opportunities possible, will prove to be brilliant. Parents in urban areas have begun sending their children to school at the age of 3, because in this competitive age they have a desire that their children be well qualified and besides that the mother often has a job outside of the home. Consequently the children are forced to begin their formal education at such a young age, being squeezed in buses like dried fish, returning home the same way. Some of them can keep up with the heavy curriculum, others cry. Some even become physically sick. According to child psychologists and child specialists it is a serious problem for children who have to carry the burden of intense study and follow different kinds of disciplines before an appropriate age. Here there is no established norm that children must wait until five years of age before starting school like in many other countries. The parents can decide, and schools will accept children of almost any age. But for whose benefit?

Children from poor families are engaged in agriculture, domestic and factory work. The child labor law forbids children under the age of 14 to work in factories, but in reality many children below this age are engaged in such work. According to a study conducted concerning the laws about child labor the following information was gathered in the industries located in Kathmandu:[9]

Type of Industry	Children below 14	Children below 18
Inside industrial districts	0.20%	0.77%
Outside industrial districts	0.42%	0.79%
Garment industry	0.28%	16.00%
Carpet industry	19.00%	33.11%

In many factories children are forced to work for low wages. In the world about 80 million children between the ages of 10 and 14 are engaged in jobs in various fields. Their physical and mental development is compromised. In the world there are about 30 million children who spend their life in the streets. The development of street children is restricted to and by their environment. What suffering must they endure? How can they look forward to a healthy, happy future?

Children's Rights

The UN declaration on the Rights of the Child was passed on November 20, 1989 by the UN General Assembly and brought the attention of the world to the needs of the child. Many countries, including Nepal, put their efforts together to pass this convention. The Convention on the Rights of the Child 1989 recognizes the necessity of giving special attention to children living in extremely difficult conditions.

---

9 Legal Research and Development Forum, Riwaj (Women's Magazine, Vol. 1, Year 1, 1991, p. 13.

It is stated in clause 2 of the convention: "All rights without exception will be available to all children and it will be the duty of the state to save them from any kind of discrimination. The state should not deprive them of any right, instead it should take positive steps to safeguard them."

With a view to adopting the convention on the rights of the child 1989, a World Summit Conference was called in New York City, USA on September 29-30, 1990 at the invitation of the UN Secretary General. Altogether 75 heads of state participated in this conference. This Summit Conference for the decade of 1990 fixed extensive targets for child welfare and development. The participating countries were asked to prepare programs for their respective countries. Nepal is a signatory to this convention and has prepared a program for the decade of 1990 despite the difficulties in implementing it.

Under the Directive Principles and Policies of the State in the Fourth Part of the Constitution of the Kingdom of Nepal 1990, clause 26, sub-clause 8 mentions: "The State shall make necessary arrangements to safeguard the rights and interests of children and shall ensure that they are not exploited and shall make gradual arrangements for free education."

- *Mother with her children, Kavre. Will she be able to educate them?*

Not only is there an urgent need for laws to ensure children's rights, but these laws must be implemented. Equally important is to bring about a change in our social outlook and concept. Although it is hard to fully implement the points included in the convention relating to children's rights, some of the targets mentioned could be put to practice to some degree through the programs of improvement.

In order to bring improvements in the condition of children and to protect their basic rights, health workers must make primary health services available with emphasis on preventive measures and by creating awareness in the field. Improvement in the condition of women and children who fall in the underprivileged class is a big challenge. From before birth the baby's health is affected by the behavior and food habits and mental condition of the mother. If the mother does not get nutritious food, the baby in her womb cannot grow properly. As a result, the child may be physically and mentally weak. Healthy citizens for tomorrow can only be envisaged if the mother herself is healthy.

In the educational development and character-building of the child, the parents, teachers, friends, family and social environment all play influential parts. In order to protect the infant and help him/her to become an active member of society, the parents, as well as society itself are equally responsible.

Political commitment is equally important. The responsibility of politicians does not end with the signing of the Convention on Child Rights. In its implementation, the activities concerning child welfare should be a national priority.

The communication media should seriously consider conducting programs on child welfare to increase popular awareness with the dissemination of relevant information.

Today's healthy and educated children are the assets of the nation. Parents should be fully informed and made aware of their responsibility to protect the rights and interests of their children because they are the ones who remain closest to them. But it is a combined effort which is needed - parents, society and the nation must all be concerned and actively involved in order that there be improvements in the field of child welfare.

Chapter 11

WOMEN AND POPULATION CONTROL

Rapid population growth has posed a serious problem in developing countries. With a rapidly growing population comes an imbalance between the country's available resources and its needs. The demands of an expanding society have a negative impact on environment which can, in turn, cause an economic crisis. The majority of the population in the developing world is dependent upon agriculture, which is labor intensive so large families are common. There is a saying that he who has a son will have prosperity. Because this concept is deeply rooted in the people, it is impossible to press for legal restrictions on population growth because every family wants sons.

According to the preliminary results of a national census conducted in 1991, Nepal's total population had reached 18,462,000. According to the 1981 census it was 15,022,000. The average annual growth rate from 1971 to 1981 was 2.66% Comparing the present census to those of the past 80 years, the population of Nepal has increased more than threefold. The recent census shows a change in the sex ratio from that of the census of 1981 when the ratio of males to females was higher 105:100, whereas the 1991 census shows the number of females to be higher. Among the total population in 1991 the number of males was 9,221,000 and that of females 9,241,000. The ratio was 99.78:100, that is 99.78 males for every 100 females. Within the decade from 1981 to 1991 the average annual population growth was 2.1%

The total land area of the country, is 147,181 sq. km. The hill region makes up 65% of the total area, the Himalayan region 18% and the lowlands or terai area, 17%. Fifty-four percent of the population live in the hilly and mountain areas. The terai which occupies only 17% of the total land area supports 46% of the population. In the past twelve years the population of the world has increased from 4 billion to 5 billion and it is estimated that in the coming ten years it will reach 6 billion. The estimated population growth in our country taking into consideration population density, birth rate and mortality rate per thousand, can be seen in the following chart:[1]

	1981	1991	2001
Density of population per sq. km.	102.1	132.4	167.2
Birth rate per thousand	44.4	37.4	30.4
Mortality rate per thousand	18.5	13.3	10.2

By 2000 AD more than half of the population of developing countries will be comprised of people under the age of 25. In the world two children are born every second which amounts to 260,000 a day. In Nepal the main reasons for population growth are:

1. Economy heavily dependent upon agriculture
2. Labour intensive agricultural system
3. Traditional religious, cultural and social values and beliefs
4. Illiteracy and ignorance
5. No recognition of women's labour
6. Limited health care services
7. Continued practice of child marriage and polygamy
8. Migration
9. Lack of women's participation

The fertility rate of Nepali women has been on average, 6 children per mother. Child marriage is still in practice and girls as young as 15 years old become mothers. They have neither the capability nor the level of consciousness necessary to take population growth as a problem. If young women give birth to children before reaching the age of 18, or before achieving their full physical development, there is a high risk to both the mother and the child.

People in rural areas do not usually practice birth control because even if one or two members are added to the family, they can somehow be accommodated until they are old enough to help with the work. There is a belief that they are born with their own fate. If in the family only daughters are born the parents will continue to have more children in the hopes of

---

1   Nepal, Population Data at a Glance, National Population Information Center, Kathmandu, 1991.

having a son. Having a son is extremely important in Nepali society, because it is the son who inherits the family property and carries on the name. And it is he who is responsible for the care of his parents until they die and it is he who must perform the ceremonies at their death and in all the years required after their death. Both superstition and a lack of education have had an impact on family size. A mother who bears a son usually commands high respect and prestige in the family. It is quite common for a mother who has had only daughters to have a co-wife. It is the chromosomes in the male semen that determines the sex of the child, but if a daughter is born it is the woman who gets all the blame and, after several daughters, her husband will take another wife in the hopes of having a son. This practice is widespread in Nepal, India, Pakistan, China and Bangladesh.

The problem of rampant population growth was mentioned in the Third Five-year Plan (1965-1970) and since then the Nepal Family Planning Association has been working in this field. The Fourth Five-Year Plan (1970-1975) and the Fifth Five Year Plan (1975-1980) emphasized the extension of the family planning program and on the planned control of migration in order to limit population growth. The Sixth Five-Year Plan (1980-1985) gave special emphasis to curb population growth. It was during this period that the National Planning Council framed its national policy on population. All the points mentioned the policy were included in the Seventh Five-year Plan (1985-1990) in toto. The Seventh Five-Year Plan, with the objective of bringing about the necessary balance in population growth and economic development, set out the following policies:

1. To fulfil the demands yet to be accomplished by extending family planning services.
2. To integrate programs related to population control in development projects with special attention given the interrelation between development and the existing population.
3. To emphasize programs concerning women's development because the status of women in society is enhanced through education and opportunities for female employment and will result in a positive impact on controlling population growth.
4. To increase the participation of the panchayat class organizations and other non-governmental organizations in population programs.
5. To control the ever increasing migration.[2]

---

2 Seventh Five-Year Plan, page 143.

According to the above policies the population control programs were coordinated with the integrated programs, with trainings and publicity provided by the National Population Commission, the Women's Development Division and health related branches under the Health Ministry. No satisfactory implementation could be achieved according to the set population policy and objectives. The expected development of human resources with the help of foreign aid was not realized.

The effective role women can play in population control has been shown in various studies. Population programs have been successful in countries where women have benefitted from development activities. The process of development and awareness has made a direct impact on population growth in Europe, USA, Japan, Denmark, and Sweden compared to the underdeveloped countries in Africa, Latin America and South Asia where population control activities have been less effective.

In 1940 in Japan the average family had five children whereas in 1967 the situation showed a drastic change as each family had only 1.69 children. Population control of this kind was made possible in part because of a proper population policy. Condoms and other methods of contraception were easily accessible. Abortion was available on demand. It was inexpensive and safe, with a large portion of the expenses covered by a national health insurance scheme.

The policy of "only one child" began in China a decade ago with the objective to reduce the population growth rate. It has come to light that in the decade 1980-1990 about 600,000 baby girls were "lost". Therefore, when developing a population policy, let the methods used in China be a warning, consider the possible effects any policy might have. According to statistics 4 out of 5 women over 25 years of age in South Asia had never gone to school. A study conducted in the Philippines established that illiterate women have, on average, four more children than those women who have had primary education. In Kenya, 22% of women who had completed 8th or 9th grade were found to be using family planning devices. In the same way, in Mexico 72% of women who had a grade 8 or 9 education were using family planning devices, whereas only 31% of women who had completed grade 5 used the devices. Only half of the women in developing countries have access to family planning devices. There are many women who do not want any more children, but contraceptive devices are unavailable. The percentage of women who do not want more children, but who are unable to obtain

A woman "taking a break" from her chores.

contraceptive devices is 77% in Africa, 57% in Asia and 43% in Latin America.[3]

In Nepal 60% of married women of childbearing age do not want another pregnancy immediately, but among them only about 17.7% use any family planning methods.[4] Even when a women wants to practice family planning she may not do so for a variety of reasons. She may not have access to consultation services, she may be too shy, or the available method may not suit her, etc. If women were sufficiently informed and involved in family planning and were self-reliant they could decide their family's size, the spacing between pregnancies, etc., on their own. It is generally acknowledged worldwide that population control is necessary to raise the economic, social and educational standard of a society. Both family and society will benefit when women are educated and can obtain economic rights. Without proper education, and knowledge of health care and nutrition, family planning will not be successful. Experience in many countries shows that even a few years of schooling has a great influence in helping women to decide their family size. Therefore, it is necessary to raise women's educational, economic and social status. Among the children in the world who cannot afford schooling the majority are girls.

In a country like Nepal where there are various ethnic groups, the publicity of family planning and the production of educational materials should be made available in the various national languages. Various family planning devices should be available to all along with educational and consultation services. The general public should be well-informed. The concept that family planning is exclusively for women should be totally rejected.

The programs conducted with a view to controlling population should not be isolated, but should be integrated into and linked with other developmental activities. Not only physicians, but health care workers, too, can play an important role in increasing people's awareness by providing basic information on the subject. Women usually remain uninformed about the programs run by governmental and non-governmental agencies. And

---

3 Population Issues Briefing Kit, United Nations Family Planning Association, 1991.
4 The Situation of Nepal's Population Information, Govinda Adhikari, paper presented at Seminar "Local Workshop for Population" - Family Planning Program, 1991.

since the basic system of communication is only through men, women have little chance of getting the right information. Until and unless both sexes are allowed to be involved in family planning education development activities, no programs will be successful.

If any woman feels that abortion is essential, it should be freely permitted. The use of unsafe and traditional abortion methods have caused innumerable deaths. Presently if a woman wants an abortion in a private clinic she will have to pay an exorbitant fee.

European women involved in the abortion rights movement participating in the European Conference on Abortion and Contraception held in Geneva in September 1992 expressed their grave concern on this subject. Abortion was taken as a routine form of birth control in east European countries, but in the present changed political context a woman's right to abortion has been under attack. In Poland abortion was easily available under a law passed in 1956. Now, the legislation appears to make abortion more difficult with a proposed ban on abortion, and with a provision for imprisonment of any doctors involved. Polish women are now going to Czech, Slovakia, Lithuania and Germany to obtain abortions.

The rate of abortion is higher in the United States than in any other developed country, even though traditionally Scandinavians have the most liberal laws. In Spain and Portugal, there is restriction on abortions for non-medical reasons. In Ireland there is an outright ban on abortions. Every year about 4,000 Irish women travel to England for an abortion. In early 1992 an Irish girl of fourteen years of age, a rape victim, was not permitted to go to England for abortion. The case gained wide publicity because the Irish Supreme Court decided not to allow her to have an abortion. In today's world population growth, widespread poverty, deterioration of environment, increasing urbanization, loss of natural resources, and growing environmental pollution, are all interrelated. To help bring harmony into all these areas it is necessary to have well-regulated family planning programs.

It is universally accepted that women's role is important in population control, but man's involvement is equally important. In developing countries, up to the present time, 75% of the women and 25% of the men have been sterilized although a vasectomy for a man is easier, faster, cheaper and safer than sterilization is for a woman. The most popular contraceptive methods used by women are the intra-uterine device (IUD), oral pills, and injection. Till now, greater stress has been given to women's involvement than to men's, but men must start to shoulder more responsibility.

There can be little effective family planning unless women's status in the family is raised, and they can have more of a say with regard to the number of children they have and the method of birth control they feel most comfortable with, including vasectomy.

Chapter 12

WOMEN AND POLITICS

The history of Nepal proudly shows that at different periods its women have contributed greatly to the awakening of political consciousness. As far back as 1814 Nepali women exhibited their strength in the historical battle of Kalanga Fort at Nalapani against the British and their cannons by using khukuris (knives) and stones.

In 1917, the first women's organization "Women's Committee" was formed in Siraha District with the purpose of making people aware of their political and social conditions. It was initiated by two very assertive women, Yogmaya Devi and Divya Devi Koirala, but it would survive for only one and a half years because the ruling authorities charged the organisation with participating in undesirable activities. It would be some time before women would again be able to establish their own organizations.

The oppressive Rana regime lasted for 104 years, until it was finally overthrown in 1951. It was the struggle in India against British colonial rule that greatly influenced the Nepali people to rise up against their oppressors during the Rana regime. The Ranas killed four freedom fighters (Sukra Raj Shastri, Dharma Bhakta, Dasharath Chandra and Gangalal) in 1940 in an effort to suppress the growing people's movement for democracy, but their action only gave the people more courage to fight.

At this time significant contributions to the movement were made by Yogmaya Devi through literature, Melawa Devi through song, Tulaja Sharma through her involvement with the Gandhi Ashram, Durga Devi Acharya Dixit through her teaching, and Moti Devi Tuladhar through her writing. In 1947 Chandra Kanta Malla (sister of the martyr Sukra Raj Shastri) opened the Kanya School for girls in Kathmandu. Again women started coming together, and in 1947 under the leadership of Mangla Devi Singh, the Nepal Mahila Sangha (Nepal Women's Association, or NWA)) was established with the purpose of attaining women's freedom and equality for the women of Nepal. It was the NWA that mobilized women to fight for women's suffrage during the first election held in 1948. In the same year, the Adarsh Mahila Samaj (Ideal Women's Association) came into existence under the leadership of Rewanta Kumari Acharya with a view to raising social and political consciousness among Nepali women.

In 1950 the All Nepali Mahila Sangha (ANWA) was established with Punya Prabha Devi as the chairperson with the purpose of raising political and social consciousness among the people. All these women's organizations worked closely with political parties opposed to the Rana regime.

After the political change of 1951 the NWA divided into two groups under the same name. A newly developed leftist faction emerged under the leadership of Kamaksha Devi.

In 1952 another women's organization, Arya Stri Samaj, was established under the leadership of Dhana Devi with the aim of protecting Nepali women from the influence of western culture.

All of these organizations were influenced by party politics. Mangala Devi's group being Congress-oriented and Kamaksha Devi's group communist-oriented, while Punya Prabha Devi's group leaned towards palace politics.

Women were represented at the national level in the election of 1958, when Dwarika Devi Thakurani won a seat in the House of Representatives and Kamal Rana was nominated to the National Assembly. In 1960 the king established the autocratic panchayat system and put a sudden stop to all associations and their activities. Women, however, remained politically active. In protest against the undemocratic royal proclamation of 1960, a group of women led by Shailaja Acharya, Gauri Rana Joshi, Kundan Pindali Sharma, Vijaya Baral Sharma, the late Sushama Koirala and Nona Koirala openly waved black flags in a public procession. For this courageous act of defiance all of these women spent three years in prison. In this act Mangala Devi Singh and Leela Koirala also played significant roles.

During the 1970's prominent women among the student leaders were Durga Acharya Ghimire, Durga Pokhrel, Sudha Koirala and Muna Devkota. Notable women fighters for democracy in 1979 were Sama Shahi, Uma Adhikari, Meena Pande, Susheela Karki, Ambika Basnet, Anar Basnet, Kavita Bhattarai, and Bina Koirala. In 1985 came Kritanjali Bhandari,

104

Krishna Amatya, Kamala Panta, and others. These women, all Congress Party supporters, fought bravely facing police batons in their struggle against the panchayat tyranny, courting arrest in the process. Among the communists, Sahana Pradhan, Shanta Manavi, Ashta Laxmi Shakya, Sadhana Adhikari, Kalyani Shah, Sushila Shrestha, Sashi Shrestha, Sita Khadka, Gaura Prasai, Shova Kuwar, Pampha Bhusal, and Sulochana Manandhar contributed to the struggle for democracy.

During the tyrannical panchayat rule after 1960 a limited number of women held government posts, yet no solid contribution was made to the status of women either economically or socially. Nepal Women's Organisation (NWO) was not autonomous, but was created by the government itself.

The Women's Decade, 1975-1985, provided us with an opportunity to take a retrospective look at the role and status of women. A three year research study started in 1979 on the status of women in Nepal was carried out to determine the actual participation and contribution of women in the rural economy, including their input in the decision-making process, their role in the social and cultural milieu, and in economic activities. One of the visible achievements of the UN Decade for Women in Nepal was the establishment of institutions for women in both the government and the NGO sector. But despite some legal reforms intending to improve women's condition, the absence of a truly democratic political environment made it difficult for people to raise a voice. There were no legal parameters allowing for open protest by any association or group of people. There was, in fact, no special difference in the working style of governmental and non-governmental organizations as the NGO's were under the thumb of the Social Services Coordination Council (SSNCC) which was under the leadership of the queen.

The people's movement of 1989 was an organized effort by the people to get rid of the panchayat system and to usher in the multiparty democratic system. Women of various regions and ideologies actively participated and contributed greatly to the success of this movement; many also died in the struggle. Among the many women who took the lead roles in various parts of the country were: Mangala Devi Singh, Shailaja Acharya, Sahana Pradhan, Leela Koirala, Suprabha Ghimire, Bishnu Waibha (Parijat), Kalayani Shah, Hisila Yami, Laxmi Karki, Meena Khadka, Meena Poudel, Susheela Karki, Kamala Panta, Neera Khanal, Kunta Sharma, Madhavi Rimal, Uma Adhikari, Bindu Rai, Jyoti Gautam, Kamala Amatya, Leela

Shrestha, Maiya Thapa, Vandana Pahari, Usha Baskota, Nisha Bhattarai, Seeta Devi Nyaupane, and Buna Regmi.

In Yadukuha, in the district of Dhanusha, there was a direct confrontation between the rural women and the policemen who had gone to disrupt the general meeting of the people. At the meeting Bhuvaneshwari Yadav and Sonavati Yadav were killed. Januka Devi also became an innocent victim. Many innocent lives were lost and numerous other women were injured by police batons and bullets. Countless women are now struggling to raise their children alone because their husbands were killed in the movement.

The Constitution of the Kingdom of Nepal, established in 1990, was promulgated as an achievement of the people's movement. This Constitution states that the sovereignty of the country is the Nepali people. This Constitution unequivocally protects the fundamental rights and freedom of every Nepali citizen. It also mandates a parliamentary form of government, constitutional monarchy and the strengthening of multiparty democracy and the system of independent judiciary. Legal rights for Nepali women to live as capable, strong and free human beings are yet to be achieved. It is, therefore, absolutely necessary to amend the laws that exist. The traditional view that women should be supported by welfare programs because they are weak and worthy of receiving consideration needs to be drastically changed. It is imperative that women use their democratic freedoms to lobby for that legal foundation. An unending struggle from a joint single platform has to continue for acquiring rights, equal opportunities and justice for women. This can be done through associations and institutions whether they are guided by political ideologies or are fighting for the social cause of women.

The most recent development in the womens' movement, is the founding of the "Women's Security Pressure Group". Greatly alarmed by the high incidence of rape and of girl and women murders, and of violence in general against women, feminists gathered together in July 1992 and formed the Women Security Pressure Group of Nepal. To date, 57 women's organizations are members, from social service to political parties and various occupational groups. This has been an historical event in the feminist movement of Nepal where women have risen above political and ideological differences and come forward in unison on a common platform. The fundamental objective of the Women Security Pressure Group Nepal is to push ahead in the legitimate struggle for the protection and enhancement of women's rights and interests against the backdrop of suffering and exploitation that our womenfolk have put up with for ages.

- The author leading a demonstration against violence against women, Kathmandu, December 2, 1992.

At the present time there are five women parliamentarians who have been elected by popular vote in the House of Representatives and three women parliamentarians who are appointed by the House of Representatives. (This is the minimum number of women parliamentarians as required by Clause 114 in the Constitution.) It would be important that they be able to present a united front on women's issues, raising above their individual party interests. Although there are women at the parliamentary level, there are very few in the district and local levels. Until women are politically involved from the grassroots all the way to the top women will not be adequately represented, and positive changes in women's lives will be difficult to obtain.

Every woman can be politically active in her own way - even if she does nothing more than vote. She should be aware of the issues, the candidates, the choices. She should realize the importance of her own vote to support those leaders who will take seriously women's issues. She can consider the opinion of her husband, as is the custom, but she should decide herself for whom she is going to vote. This is her political responsibility both to herself and to other women.

Chapter 13

WOMEN AND LAW

Background

Nepal was made up of many independent kingdoms, until the king of one of them conquered them all in 1768. In 1847 a palace courtier snatched power from the king in a coup and all subsequent kings were held hostage for 104 years while the Ranas, as prime ministers, ruled the country. Influenced by the British, after a visit to England, the first Rana prime minister established the first civil law in 1853 which was based on Hindu scriptures.

It was only in 1948, three years after India gained her independence from British colonial rule, near the end of the 104-year Rana regime that a constitution was drawn up in an effort to pacify the growing opposition to the regime. When women were debarred voting in the election of the Kathmandu municipality in the same year despite the provision which allowed franchise for all adults without discrimination as to sex, women from the Nepal Mahila Sangh (Nepal Women's Association) dared to raise their voice and picketed in front of the residence of the then prime minister and as a result they were able to obtain their voting rights from that election on.

In 1951 the Ranas were overthrown by the people and an interim government took over under the king. In 1958 the Congress government was elected and ruled for 18 months. In 1960 the king dissolved the Parliament and banned all political parties. In 1962 a new constitution was put forward which emphasized a partyless (or one-party) panchyat system. In 1963 civil code was introduced which tried to abolish social evils such as the caste system, untouchability, child marriage, polygamy, and incompatible marriage (with 20 years or more difference in age in the couple).

The sixth amendment of the civil code in 1975 brought about the following changes in the law:

- Women, who were not previously allowed alimony at their divorce, are now entitled to alimony for a period of five years or until they remarry. They are also allowed custody of their children as long as they do not marry.

- An unmarried daughter thirty-five years and older is entitled to an equal share of parental property, but if she gets married after the age of 35 she must forfeit the property.

- The penalty for polygamy or bigamy was increased.
- Previously, a daughter was not entitled to inherit the parental property if husband, wife, son, son's son and other male relatives of the deceased were surviving. Now, a daughter is entitled to inherit in the absence of husband, wife, son or son's son. Other male relatives of the deceased cannot claim any right to property as long as the daughter of the deceased is surviving.

- Adoption of a female child is now legal.

- The penalty for human trafficking was increased to ten years imprisonment if caught before he/she has effected a sale. the penalty was increased to twenty years if he/she is caught after a sale has been effected.

- A rapist is punished with imprisonment ranging from three to ten years. In addition, half the property of the rapist will be forfeited and given to the rape victim. The law also grants the right of self-defence to the victim if she kills the rapist within an hour of the act. If she kills the rapist after the expiry of an hour of the crime the victim can herself be punished with a fine of up to Rs. 5000 or a sentence up to ten year's imprisonment.

During the panchyat system there was a centralization of power in the palace. This system was thrown over by the people's movement in 1989.

The Constitution of the Kingdom of Nepal, 1990

The present constitution is the accomplishment of the People's Movement of 1989. After a continuous 30-year struggle the Nepali people were finally successful in establishing a democracy. State power is now with the people. Human rights, adult franchise, a parliamentary system of government, and a constitutional monarchy are the chief features of the constitution. In order to transform the all-powerful, absolute monarchy into a constitutional monarchy great sacrifices had to be made by the Nepali people so dedicated to freedom and democracy. The constitution is for conducting a state which operates with equal justice for all and it is the country's main legal document.

The Constitution of the Kingdom of Nepal 1990 stipulates "All citizens shall be equal before the law. No person shall be denied the equal protection of the law. No discrimination shall be made against any citizen in the application of general laws on grounds of religion, race, sex, caste, tribe or ideological conviction or any of these. No citizen shall be discriminated against on the basis of caste, as untouchable, or be denied access to any public place, or be deprived of the use of public utilities. Any contravention of this provision shall be punishable by law. No discrimination in regard to remuneration shall be made between men and women for the same work."[1] Sub-clause 3 of clause 11 clearly states the provisions for the protection and advancement of the interests of women, children, the aged and those who are physically or mentally incapacitated or those who belong to a class which is economically, socially or educationally under-developed. The Preamble of the Constitution has guaranteed fundamental human rights to Nepali citizens on the basis of freedom and equality and promoted amongst the people of Nepal the spirit of fraternity and the bond of unity. The fundamental rights as set down in the Constitution safeguard freedom of thought and expression, freedom of opening up organizations, freedom of gathering peacefully, freedom to take up any profession, industry or trade.

According to sub-clause 6 of clause 45 of the constitution every Nepali citizen who has attained the age of 18 shall be entitled to vote in one of the election constituencies in accordance with the provisions of law. Sub-clause 7 contains the provision that every person entitled to vote in the elections for the House of Representatives may be a candidate from any of the election constituencies subject to the provisions of the existing laws.

The term "every Nepali citizen" clearly means that there is no discrimination allowed on the basis of sex. Besides this, in order to increase the political participation of women, at least 5% of the total number of candidates contesting an election from any party to the House of

---

1   Constitution of the Kingdom of Nepal, 1990, part 3.

Representatives must be women.[2] When the National Assembly is formed by the House of Representatives at least 3 of the 35 members, elected on the principle of proportional representation, have to be women. This reservation is necessary until such time as all of our womenfolk are politically aware and active in politics.

The Constitution has specific provisions against exploitation and discrimination and confirms equal protection of all citizens under the law. Yet the Civil Code of 1963 has, in fact, discriminated against women in many ways, especially with regards to ownership of property.

Clause 4 of the Constitution states that Nepal is a Hindu Kingdom. Religion, however, is an individual affair, and not a subject to be imposed by the state. Proclaiming Nepal to be a Hindu State may create religious, social, cultural and communal tension. The Constitution of the Kingdom of Nepal, 1958 was silent on the subject of religion, whereas the present Constitution, made after a lapse of thirty-two years, has accepted the concept of a religious state. Religious freedom is also a part of human rights.

Many aspects of Hinduism have added to the exploitation of women. In relation to citizenship, the Constitution has maintained a policy of discrimination against women. A foreign woman married to a Nepali citizen, after she starts proceedings to renounce her foreign citizenship shall get Nepali citizenship.[3] But if a Nepali woman marries a foreign citizen, the husband not only cannot get Nepali citizenship, but he is lucky if he can even get a visa to stay in the country. Concerning the property rights, clause 17 of the Constitution has stated that all citizens shall, subject to the existing laws, have the right to acquire, win, sell and otherwise manage property. Yet in practice the existing laws are contrary to the Constitution. Since women are allowed property rights only in extreme and unusual cases.

Existing Laws and Women

Most of the present laws have been in existence since the Civil Code of 1963 and are incompatible with the provisions in the Constitution of the Kingdom of Nepal 1990 and they still discriminate against women. Nepal has signed the United Nations Convention on the Elimination of All Forms of Discrimination Against Women. This convention states that

---

2   The Constitution of the Kingdom of Nepal, 1990, Clause 114.
3   Ibid, Clause 9.

"Discrimination against women" implies any distinction exclusion or restriction made on the basis of sex which denies women their human rights and fundamental freedoms. (Article 1) A policy of eliminating discrimination against women and ensuring equality will be pursued through appropriate constitutional and legislative provisions covering discrimination by individuals, agencies or through existing laws, regulations, customs and practices.

In our context, despite the amendments made from time to time the Civil Code of 1963 needs to be amended completely. In section 16, under the heading "Of Partition of Property" of the civil code an unmarried daughter can acquire a share of her parent's property just as a son, but only after reaching the age of 35 years. After inheriting her share of property if she gets married or elopes her inherited property will be seized by the nearest co-parcener of the father's line after deducting her marriage expenses and dowry. The wife cannot live separately taking her share of property during the lifetime of her husband without his consent. The husband is liable to provide food and clothing to this wife and sons according to his income and prestige, but there is no legal provision in the code for a daughter, even for basic maintenance. In this way women are made dependent on men. A widow cannot claim for partition of property until she reaches the age of 30, until which time her husband's coparcener gives her food and clothes according to his status and allows her to perform her religious duties.[4] According to section 10 of the partition of property a married woman can live separately without showing any cause if she has completed the age of 35 years and has completed 15 years of marriage.

According to section 1 of the chapter "Of Intestate Succession", the rightful heir means the nearest successor on the male line within seven generations. When somebody dies without leaving a will, the daughter does not get such property if the dead person's husband, wife, son or son's son are living.

"Stridhana", in section 14 of the chapter " Of Woman's Property" states that a woman has an absolute right to hold and dispose of her self-earned property. According to the aforesaid law a woman has an absolute right to three kinds of property of her own which are known as:

1.   "Daijo" (dowry) which she receives from her parent's side.

---

4   Civil Code of Laws, clause 13.

2. "Pewa" (property received from husband and from his family's side).
3. Her savings and self-earned property.

The immovable property of "pewa" must be in a written form. But a woman may not claim her daijo or pewa from her joint family properties unless she produces the written documents made by the coparcener with the consent of those who have completed the age of 16. It means she will not be able to claim money spent by her husband or his family as daijo and pewa without the requisite documents in that regard. The heir of a woman's property shall be a son who is staying with her; if there is no such son then a son who is living separately; if she has no son, her husband will get it; if she has no husband living, her unmarried daughter will have the property. In case she has no unmarried daughter, it will go to her married daughter. If she has no married daughter it will go to her son's son, and if none of them exists the rightful person will get the property according to law.[5]

A woman inherits her share of property from the share of her husband. According to the law of inheritance the property should be shared among father, mother, wife and son. This means father, mother and sons are coparcener of the inheritance property. A woman can claim her right to property only as somebody's wife. She can neither possess any property independently, nor, in times of need, can her share of marriage property be separated and used by her. In the joint family the husband alone can be the inheritor of property and not his wife. A woman gets her share when she becomes a widow in the joint family. Meanwhile, she gets only what her husband gives her as long as she remains at home as his wife. If she stays separate from him she will receive her portion only with his consent.

According to clause 9 relating to borrowing and lending, any male or female as the head of the household is an adult who has settled down looking after the house, agricultural land, trade or occupation. Without the written consent of father or husband, the wife's transaction will not be acceptable. In practice women are rarely accepted as heads of households. Under the existing legal system it is almost impossible for women to get their share of inheritance through a court of law as the property almost always goes to the "rightful heir" - the men. Thus women are forced to live under domination and do not dare to divorce their husbands even if they are tortured.

---

5   Civil Code of Laws, 1963, Clause 14 on woman's inherited property.

Under section 9 of the chapter on marriage no man can marry another's wife or keep another woman as wife when his wife is still living or until the husband and the wife are legally separated, except under the following conditions:

- when his wife has an incurable sexually transmitted disease
- when the wife goes insane and there is no hope of recovery
- when no child is born (or was born and dies) within ten years of marriage
- when the wife becomes blind
- when the wife stays separately with her share of property according to section 10 and section 10 (a) of the chapter "on partition of property"

How far is it justifiable for a husband to have a second marriage in the above conditions? Is the wife alone accountable for not bearing any child, or getting an incurable disease, going insane, being blind or for the death of her children? What should be done when these conditions fall on a man? The law is unequivocally on the side of men and defies the Constitution which advocates equality. If any man except on the above mentioned conditions, marries a second time or keeps a second wife he will be jailed for 1-2 months and fined Rs. 1,000-2,000 rupees. If a woman knowingly marries in the same way or agrees to be kept as a wife she will also be punished in the same way.

Tenancy rights are enjoyed only by the husband, wife, and sons only. A widowed daughter-in-law or unmarried daughter cannot claim tenancy rights.[6]

Despite the Constitution's stipulation that no one will be discriminated against, and everyone shall receive equal protection under the law, the existing discriminatory laws have not yet been amended. The legal system, based on traditional Hindu concepts, is responsible for the unequal social and economic conditions between men and women. Together with bringing about a change in the legal system, social concept must also be changed. The formulation of laws should be for justice and the people should have a natural right to self-respect. Although woman's responsibility is great, the discriminatory provisions of law have prevented her from working independently. Only when women are strong within the family will positive

---

6   Land Act, 1964, Section 26.

changes be seen in society. There are also men who feel threatened by women who are capable and strong. Asking for equality is not a call for competition. It is quite natural for women to enjoy the right to live as human beings. The pressure of discriminating between the son and the daughter from birth is the product of traditional social concepts and superstitions. For some years to come the state should follow a system of reservation in order to increase the participation of women in the fields of education, employment, and politics as well as in public life. Until and unless women get economic rights they will always be forced to lead a dependent life. Special attention to women's education is of utmost importance in order for them to be able to use the available opportunities. There will be no change in social attitudes as long as the discriminatory laws exist. All unequal and discriminatory laws should be amended on the basis of the principle of equality as advocated in the Constitution of the Kingdom of Nepal, 1990.

Chapter 14

WOMEN AND ORGANIZATIONS

Women's organizations and institutions have been working in Nepal for a long time. If we look at their history we find many organizations that were formed along social as well as political lines, although the tyrannical government kept a tight rein on their activities. At the call of the United Nations, Women's Year was observed in 1975. In connection with the Women's Decade, 1975-1985 women's programs began in governmental and non-governmental fields. After the people's struggle for democracy in 1989, the banned political organizations and institutions related to women were revived and reorganized. In the social field, organizations and institutions were widely established. The organizations and institutions related to women that are in existence at the present time can be divided into the following categories: political, social and governmental.[1] These will be discussed each in turn.

POLITICAL

The Nepal Women's Association (NWA)

NWA was established in 1947 with a view to achieving women's freedom and equality. The founding and present chairperson is Mangala Devi Singh. It has recognized economic safeguards as the first step in safeguarding women's rights and interests. Functioning during the Rana period's feudal administrative system, it remained a democratic organization fighting for women's awakening. It played a special role in the revolution of 1951 and was active until it was banned in 1980. It played a very important role in the people's struggle which began on February 18, 1989. Its activities have increased since the establishment of democracy and it is working in close association with the Nepali Congress Party.

---

1   The sections and branch offices established on the government level.

All Nepal Women Association (ANWA)

After ideological differences with NWA, ANWA was established with a view to achieving women's freedom and equality in 1952 under the leadership of the late Kamaksha Devi. The Association was banned by the anti-democratic forces in 1961. In 1981 this association was re-organized under the leadership of Shanta Manavi. It played an important role in the people's struggle which began in February 1989 and since has extended its program throughout the country. This association is closely related to the Nepal Communist Party - United Marxists and Leninists. The present chairperson of this association is Sahana Pradhan.

National Women's Forum (NWF)

In 1990 this association was established under the leadership of the present chairperson, Tula Rana, with the objective of providing economic, social and political rights to women. NWF conducts its activities as an associate organization of the National Democratic Party which is headed by the former panchayat leaders.

Mothers' Club

In the context of Women's Year in 1975, this center was started by the Nepal Red Cross Society under the leadership of the late Princess Princep Shah. Family welfare related programs are carried out with the objective of raising family living standards. The present chairperson is Shanti Parajuli.

Business and Professional Women's Club (BPWC)

This club was established under the leadership of the present chairperson, Ambika Shrestha, in 1974 with a view to making job opportunities available to educated unemployed women in various professions for their economic, social and intellectual development. One of its major accomplishments has been to set up free day care centers for the children (under five years of age) of women working in the industrial areas of Patan, Balaju, Hetauda and Pokhara. It also provides training sessions related to secretarial and managerial services for women.

Women's Development Center (WDC)

WDC was established in Nepalganj in 1977 by Rina Tulachan. Its purpose is to remove superstitious beliefs existing in the social customs and manners regarding women. Integrated programs are conducted through this center. The present chairperson is Purnawati Sherchan.

Women's Welfare Center (WWC)

WWC was established by the late Shanti Subba in Jhapa in 1978 with the objective of awakening among women a feeling of social progress and understanding. Family welfare projects are run by this center for underdeveloped ethnic communities.

Women's Development Organization (WDO)

WDO was founded in Biratnagar in 1978 by Susheela Chapagain, who is the present chairperson. According to its target of income generation for women, the organization helps them to become self-reliant through its different activities.

Center for Women and Development (CWD)

Established in 1983 by Bina Pradhan with the purpose of mobilizing the full participation of women in development work, CWD has conducted studies, research and professional training sessions for women as well as carried out evaluation on the effectiveness of development activities as per the demand of other organizations. It provides ten-month training courses on communication education for women. CWD maintains a library with magazines and journals about women, and publishes "The Networker", a trimesterly magazine in English which focuses on issues from a women's perspective. The present chairperson is Prabha Thakar.

ABC Nepal

In 1987 ABC Nepal (Agro-forestry Basic Health and Co-operatives) was established with the aim of bringing about the development of agriculture, forestry, basic health care and the concept of cooperatives with women's participation. It has been creating an awareness about trafficking of girls and women. The founder and present chairperson of this organization is Durga Ghimire.

Creative Development Center (CDC)

CDC was established in 1988 with the objective of creating a new alternative for the underdeveloped rural ethic communities and especially for the exploited and harassed women. Through this center the Tharu and other under-privileged women have been served. The founder chairperson of this organization is Shanti Chaudhari.

Legal Aid and Consultancy Center

Established in 1987 with the objective of safeguarding the rights and interests of women and children, this center conducts legal and literacy programs in rural areas. Legal consultation is provided for women, with the special facility of consultation by telephone for those women who cannot leave their homes. The center's founder and chairperson is Shanta Thapaliya.

Women Entrepreneur Association of Nepal (WEAN)

Started in 1988 by a group of women entrepreneurs, WEAN tries to develop the entrepreneurial skills of other women throughout the country. The founder and present chairperson is Yangzi Sherpa.

Women and Environment (WE)

WE has been running integrated programs to create environmental consciousness. It has provided environmental education in some schools. The group's founder/president is Kamala Dhungel.

Service for Unprivileged Section of Society (SUSS)

SUSS has been running as a service center for the helpless since 1989 with the objective of increasing women's awareness of the constitution and laws, especially those relevant to women.   An additional objective is to conduct research studies on women's problems for publication.   This organization was established under the leadership of Shilu Singh, who continues to play an active role.

Women's Awareness Center Nepal (WACN)

WACN (pronounced "waken") was established in 1991 with a view to enhancing the inherent capabilities and power in women for their all-round development as well as for the well-being of their children and families. Emphasis is given to integrated community programs and training on gender issues. This organization was established under the present chairperson, Prativa Subedi.

Nepal Center for Women and Children Affairs (NCWCA)

In 1989 NWCA was established with the objective of bringing about legal reform in order to remove discrimination against women and children. The founder and present chairperson of this center is Kusum Sakha.

Stri Shakti (S2)

Stri Shakti was established with a view to empowering women and making them self-reliant. It has been running a half-way house for destitute women whom they encourage by providing training to enable them to obtain employment. It is presently conducting research on the status of Nepali women in this regard. The founder and present chairperson is Indira Shrestha.

Women's Rehabilitation Center

In 1990 this center was established in order to rehabilitate women who have been rescued from prostitution and those who have AIDS. The founder and present chairperson of this center is Renu Rajbhandari.

Women in Development, Nepal (WID)

WID was established in 1990 with the objective of involving women in the mainstream of national development by increasing rural women's active participation. The founding and present chairman is Purusottam Risal.

Association of Craft Producers (ACP)

Established in 1984, ACP is a private, professional, non-profit organization to provide design, market, technical and managerial services to low-income female craft producers. The founding member and present executive director is Meera Bhattari.

Technical and Skill Development Center for Blind and Disabled

This center was established with the objective to eliminate the misconception towards the blind and disabled as the curse of the gods and to prove their capabilities even in technical fields. The founder member and present executive director is Shashi Kala Singh.

Child Workers in Nepal (CWIN)

Established in 1987, CWIN plays an advocacy role for the rights, welfare and dignity of the child, and gives special attention to addressing the problems of child labor and children at risk at the local, regional and national levels. It has recently established an emergency shelter for girls at risk and provides for their education. Its magazines are published in both English and Nepali. Gauri Pradhan is the founding member and present executive director of CWIN.

GOVERNMENTAL
Divisions, Sections and Projects

Women's Training Center (WTC)

WTC was established in Kathmandu in 1961. In 1975, in connection with the UN Women's Year, women's training centers were opened up in Pokhara, Surkhet, Dhankutta and Dipayal. Its target is to develop rural women, to prepare necessary manpower according to the political system, and to train them to assume leadership assignments. This training center is under the Ministry of Local Development. The director is Dhunu Rana.

Women's Development Division (WDD)

WDD was established in 1980 with the main objective of removing the distance between the experts in development and the rural women. Loans are provided to rural women on collective security by coordinating various banks under the "Production Credit for Rural Women". The PCRW project aims to give access to credit to poor rural women in combination with community development activities. Its objective is to save women's labor and time under community development programs. Since 1989 it has been working under the Ministry of Local Development. Chadani Joshi played a leading role in the initiation of this program.

Women's Development Division (Focal Point)

This division was organized in 1987 under the Labor and Social Welfare Ministry. Besides working as the national focal point of SAARC, its objectives are to coordinate the activities of other ministerial women-related activities, frame policies at a national level and collect statistics. The women involved with this branch from its inception are Prabha Basnet and Chapala Pande.

Women's Education Project

The main objective of this project which began in 1970 is to mobilize women's participation by providing training opportunities in order to include women in the education profession, especially in primary schools situated in the remote districts of the country. A School Leaving Certificate (SLC) is required before one is eligible for the training. The educational qualification is fixed according to the needs of the area. A special program for girls is running under this project for those girls who were unable to get their SLC. Neelam Basnet has played a leading role since its inception.

Small Farming Women's Program (SFWP)

In 1975 the Agricultural Development Bank, with an objective of bringing about an improvement in the living standards of small farmers, implemented the Small Farmers Development Project (SFDP) in Dhanusha and Nuwakot districts. SFWP was started in 1981 to give priority to the women of small farming communities. In order to bring about a qualitative improvement in the rural women's condition, agricultural loans were provided, and economic social and community activities were conducted.

SFDP is presently functioning in all 75 districts of the Kingdom, and SFWP is running in 43 districts. The director of this program is Indu Pant.

Women and Development Studies

Since 1987, under the Home Science Department of Padma Kanya Campus, a course on "Women in Development" has been included in the curriculum. Its objective is to examine various aspects of women and development and to conduct studies which have helped in making plans and implementing them for women's advancement. Dr. Leela Devi K.C. is the head of this program.

OTHER ORGANIZATIONS

Women's Emergency Center, Chitwan
Rural Women's Welfare Center, Kabhre
Women's Development Center, Nuwakot
Women's Inspiration Center, Kathmandu
Kathmandu Rural Women's Development Club, Lalitpur
Women's Inspiration Center, Kathmandu
Women's Welfare Center, Kathmandu
Nepal Women's Welfare Society, Kathmandu
Women's Legal Profession Organization, Kathmandu
Peaceful Women's Service Center, Lamjung
Nepal Women's Welfare Center, Dharan
Women's Development Service Center, Dhanusha

* * * * *

In this way, the organizations and institutions relating to women have been helping to increase the involvement of women in social, economic and political fields. The political associations are capable of spreading their network throughout the country, yet they tend to be rather more active only during elections. Firstly, their aim is to achieve certain political objectives and, secondly, they work as a support to one or another political party. It is natural that they support their respective parties, but for the real problems facing women there should be an atmosphere in which all women, regardless of party affiliation, are ready to speak with one voice. It is necessary to have a committee represented by all in order to speak unitedly in addressing women's common problems. The history of the world does not provide us with any definite evidence that women's development is possible only within a particular political system. In our context, the change in the political system has come about according to the desire of the people. In the evolution of this system and in the development of underpriviliged groups, particularly those of women, the political and social organizations related to women have to come together on many points according to the circumstances.

These organizations have sprung up with the feeling of working for women's progress. If these organizations and institutions move ahead with the participation of local women they can achieve long-lasting progress. There should be regular supervision of the work done by organizations and a national policy should be formulated, so that these organizations do not take deceitful advantage of the situation for their own self-interest in the name of women's development.

Some foreign non-governmental organizations give economic assistance to programs relating to women. It is not easy, however, for organizations outside the Kathmandu area to establish contact with and work according to the dictates of a donor agency. Even the social organizations under the Social Services National Coordination Council (SSNCC), now known as the Social Welfare Council (SWC) have felt the lack of coordination as SWC tends to control more than coordinate. It is up to the council to remove this impression. The crucial problem today is that some organizations are guided by their own narrow self-interests and motives, whereas some others are doing exceptional work. There is, in fact, an apparent lack of coordination between organizations that work properly and the donor agencies that have a sincere desire to assist. In this field also the practice of giving priority to one's own people is widespread.

The press also has been contributing to the female awakening. Among the prominent Nepali women-oriented papers are Asmita, Nari Manch, Riwaj and Richa. Articles and essays on women also appear in various other weeklies and monthlies. When we analyze women's situation and status today we cannot separate it from the economic, social and political system. There is a special role of culture and religion together with the country's geographical features, natural resources and the size of population on the condition of any special class or inhabitant. Various ethnic communities and different geographical and cultural regions exhibit a wide variety of social values and cultural beliefs. And yet, women are left behind in every field. Even poverty itself has been womanized. In this situation the women-related associations and organizations have a very challenging role to play.

124